The Ultimate

Air Fryer

Cookbook

2000 Days of Creative and Flavorful Recipes to Transform Your Cooking Style

Elizabeth S. Levesque

Editor: AALIYAH LYONS

Interior Design: BROOKE WHITE

Cover Art: DANIELLE REES

Food stylist: SIENNA ADAMS

Table Of Contents

Introduction

Welcome to "The Ultimate Air Fryer Cookbook." In a world where culinary innovation and efficiency have become the order of the day, the air fryer has taken center stage in kitchens across the globe. Its ability to create delectable, crispy dishes with significantly less oil has revolutionized the way we cook and eat. If you've just unboxed your air fryer or you've been using it for some time, this book is here to guide you on an exciting culinary journey, unlocking the full potential of this remarkable kitchen appliance.

As we dive into the world of air frying, it's important to understand the basics. The air fryer is not a magic wand, but rather a culinary tool that uses hot air to cook food quickly and evenly. With a convection fan, your ingredients are enveloped in a whirlwind of hot air, producing the satisfying crunch we all love, while using only a fraction of the oil that traditional frying methods require. This method of cooking is not only healthier but also incredibly versatile, allowing you to prepare a wide variety of dishes, from crispy fries to succulent chicken wings, and even mouthwatering desserts.

In "The Ultimate Air Fryer Cookbook," we will not only explore the endless possibilities of this appliance but also provide you with a comprehensive guide to mastering its use. We will start with the essentials, discussing the different types of air fryers available on the market, their features, and how to choose the one that suits your needs. Whether you have a countertop model or a built-in oven with an air frying function, this book has you covered.

Why the air fryer, you might ask? For starters, it's a kitchen gadget that has taken the culinary world by storm in recent years. Its popularity can be attributed to a few key factors: speed, health-conscious cooking, and, of course, its cost-effectiveness. By harnessing the power of hot air circulation, air fryers cook food with little to no oil, producing dishes that are both delicious and healthy. And, let's not forget, they do it all in a fraction of the time it takes traditional cooking methods. It's a kitchen revolution that anyone on a budget can embrace.

Now, let's discuss how to use this cookbook to its fullest potential:

Getting to Know Your Air Fryer: Before you embark on your air frying adventure, take the time to familiarize yourself with your machine. Read the instruction manual, understand its temperature and time settings, and learn how to preheat it. These initial steps will ensure you get the best results from your air fryer.

Essential Tips and Tricks: Our cookbook contains a dedicated section on tips and tricks to elevate your air frying game. Discover the secrets to achieving that perfect golden crisp and ensuring that your food is cooked evenly every time. From shaking the basket at the right intervals to experimenting with different cooking temperatures, we've got you covered.

Understanding Ingredients: Every ingredient behaves differently in the air fryer. In this book, we've provided insights into how various ingredients cook in the air fryer, ensuring that you can adapt your favorite recipes or create new ones with confidence.

Delicious and Diverse Recipes: "The Ultimate Air Fryer Cookbook" is a treasure trove of recipes that cater to every palate and dietary preference. Whether you're a carnivore, a vegetarian, or have specific dietary requirements, you'll find a wealth of recipes that are easy to follow and deliver mouthwatering results. From classic comfort foods like crispy chicken tenders and onion rings to health-conscious options such as vegetable spring rolls and baked sweet potato fries, we've got something for everyone.

Cooking for Every Occasion: This cookbook will take you on a culinary journey for every occasion. From weeknight dinners to weekend brunches, holiday feasts to casual gatherings with friends, you'll find recipes that suit the moment. Explore a range of dishes that will make you the star of any gathering, from appetizers to main courses, and don't forget to save room for dessert.

Customization and Creativity: One of the most exciting aspects of air frying is the flexibility it offers in creating your own dishes. We encourage you to experiment with flavors, ingredients, and cooking techniques. In this book, we provide a solid foundation, but feel free to build upon it with your creativity.

Healthier Choices: For those who are health-conscious or looking to reduce calorie intake, we've included recipes that focus on lighter, lower-calorie options. You can enjoy the flavors you love without compromising on your health goals.

Time-Saving Solutions: We understand that in today's fast-paced world, time is a precious commodity. That's why we've included recipes that can be prepared in a jiffy. Discover quick and easy recipes that will get a delicious meal on the table in no time.

Menu Planning: Our cookbook provides suggestions for menu planning, helping you create well-rounded meals with complimentary dishes. Mix and match recipes to create the perfect combinations for your family and friends.

Conversion Charts and Cooking Times: Don't worry if your air fryer uses a different unit of measurement or has slightly different temperature settings. We've included conversion charts and guidelines for cooking times to make your cooking experience smooth and hassle-free.

"The Ultimate Air Fryer Cookbook" is not just a collection of recipes; it's your guide to embracing the incredible world of air frying. This book is designed to help you master your air fryer, no matter your level of experience in the kitchen. Whether you're a beginner or an experienced chef, you'll find something here to inspire and delight your taste buds.

Air frying is more than just a cooking method; it's a lifestyle that allows you to savor the flavors you love without compromising on health. So, let's embark on this culinary adventure together, and explore the endless possibilities that your air fryer can offer.

Happy cooking, and may your air-fried creations be both delightful and delicious!

Bon appétit!

Air Fryer Cooking Chart

Beef					
Item	Temp (°F)	Time (mins)	Item	Temp (°F)	Time (mins)
Beef Eye Round Roast (4 lbs.)	400 °F	45 to 55	Meatballs (1-inch)	370 °F	7
Burger Patty (4 oz.)	370 °F	16 to 20	Meatballs (3-inch)	380 °F	10
Filet Mignon (8 oz.)	400 °F	18	Ribeye, bone-in (1-inch, 8 oz)	400 °F	10 to 15
Flank Steak (1.5 lbs.)	400 °F	12	Sirloin steaks (1-inch, 12 oz)	400 °F	9 to 14
Flank Steak (2 lbs.)	400 °F	20 to 28			

Chicken					
Item	Temp (°F)	Time (mins)	Item	Temp (°F)	Time (mins)
Breasts, bone in (1 1/4 lb.)	370 °F	25	Legs, bone-in lb.)	380 °F	30
Breasts, boneless (4 oz)	380 °F	12	Thighs, boneless (1 1/2 lb.)	380 °F	18 to 20
Drumsticks (2 1/2 lb.)	370 °F	20	Wings (2 lb.)	400 °F	12
Game Hen (halved 2 lb.)	390 °F	20	Whole Chicken	360 °F	75
Thighs, bone-in (2 lb.)	380 °F	22	Tenders	360 °F	8 to 10

Pork & Lamb					
Item	Temp (°F)	Time (mins)	Item	Temp (°F)	Time (mins)
Bacon (regular)	400 °F	5 to 7	Pork Tenderloin	370 °F	15
Bacon (thick cut)	400 °F	6 to 10	Sausages	380 °F	15
Pork Loin (2 lb.)	360 °F	55	Lamb Loin Chops (1-inch thick)	400 °F	8 to 12
Pork Chops, bone in (1-inch, 6.5 oz)	400 °F	12	Rack of Lamb (1.5 - lb.)	380 °F	22
Flank Steak (2 lbs.)	400 °F	20 to 28			

Fish & Seafood					
Item	Temp (°F)	Time (mins)	Item	Temp (°F)	Time (mins)
Calamari (8 oz)	400 °F	4	Tuna Steak	400 °F	7 to 10
Fish Fillet (1-inch, 8 oz)	400 °F	10	Scallops	400 °F	5 to 7
Salmon, fillet (6 oz)	380 °F	12	Shrimp	400 °F	5
Swordfish steak	400 °F	10	Sirloin steaks (1-inch, 12 oz)	400 °F	9 to 14
Flank Steak (2 lbs.)	400 °F	20 to 28			

Vegetables					
INGREDIENT	AMOUNT	PREPARATION	OIL	TEMP	COOK TIME
Asparagus	2 bunches	Cut in half, trim stems	2 Tbsp	420°F	12-15 mins
Beets	1 1/2 lbs	Peel, cut in 1/2-inch cubes	1Tbsp	390°F	28-30 mins
Bell peppers (for roasting)	4 peppers	Cut in quarters, remove seeds	1Tbsp	400°F	15-20 mins
Broccoli	1 large head	Cut in 1-2-inch florets	1Tbsp	400°F	15-20 mins
Brussels sprouts	1lb	Cut in half, re-move stems	1Tbsp	425°F	15-20 mins
Carrots	1lb	Peel, cut in 1/4-inch rounds	1 Tbsp	425°F	10-15 mins
Cauliflower	1 head	Cut in 1-2-inch florets	2 Tbsp	400°F	20-22 mins
Corn on the cob	7 ears	Whole ears, remove husks	1 Tbps	400°F	14-17 mins
Green beans	1 bag (12 oz)	Trim	1 Tbps	420°F	18-20 mins
Kale (for chips)	4 OZ	Tear into pieces, remove stems	None	325°F	5-8 mins
Mushrooms	16 OZ	Rinse, slice thinly	1 Tbps	390°F	25-30 mins
Potatoes, russet	1 1/2 lbs	Cut in 1-inch wedges	1 Tbps	390°F	25-30 mins
Potatoes, russet	1lb	Hand-cut fries, soak 30 mins in cold water, then pat dry	1/2 -3 Tbps	400°F	25-28 mins
Potatoes, sweet	1lb	Hand-cut fries, soak 30 mins in cold water, then pat dry	1 Tbps	400°F	25-28 mins
Zucchini	1lb	Cut in eighths lengthwise, then cut in half	1 Tbps	400°F	15-20 mins

Chapter 1

Breakfasts

Egg & Bacon Breakfast Muffins

Prep time: 5 minutes | Cooking time: 25 minutes | Serves 4

- 4 medium eggs
- 4 slices of bacon or bacon
- 4 tsp melted butter
- 1 slice of cheese
- 2 slices of cheese
- 4 paper aluminum muffin tin
- salt and pepper to taste

1. Preheat the air fryer to 350 °F. Put the bacon slices in a frying air fryer and cook over medium heat. Bake until the slice is equally brown everywhere. Remove the bacon from the air fryer and wrap the bacon slices in the muffin molds.
2. Place a tsp of melted butter in the bottom of each mold. Beat the eggs in a bowl and add salt and pepper to taste. Now put the eggs in the muffin molds.
3. Place the molds on a rack and place in the air fryer. Bake the bacon and egg muffins for 10 to 15 minutes in the preheated air fryer. When the muffins are almost ready, place the 1/2 slice of cheese on top of each muffin and bake them in the air fryer for a few minutes until the cheese has melted.

Meat Pizza

Prep time: 10 minutes | Cook time: 15 minutes | Serves 2

- 8 oz ground beef
- 1 tablespoon marinara sauce
- ½ teaspoon dried oregano
- 1/3 cup Cheddar cheese, shredded
- ½ teaspoon coconut oil, melted
- ¼ teaspoon dried cilantro

1. Mix ground beef with dried cilantro and dried oregano.
2. Brush the air fryer basket with coconut oil.
3. Make 2 flat balls from the ground beef and put them in the air fryer basket.
4. Top them with marinara sauce and Cheddar cheese.
5. Cook the pizza at 375°F for 15 minutes.

Sweet Buns

Prep time: 10 minutes | Cook time: 12 minutes | Serves 2

- 2 tablespoons coconut flour
- ¼ teaspoon baking powder
- 1 teaspoon Erythritol
- 1 teaspoon mascarpone
- 1 teaspoon coconut oil, melted
- 2 eggs, beaten
- ¼ cup Mozzarella, shredded
- 1 teaspoon avocado oil

1. Mix all ingredients in the mixing bowl and knead the dough.
2. Make the small buns and put them in the air fryer.
3. Bake the buns at 375°F for 12 minutes or until they are light brown.

Dill Egg Rolls

Prep time:10 minutes |Cook time: 4 minutes |Serves 4

- 2 eggs, hard-boiled, peeled
- 1 tablespoon cream cheese
- 1 tablespoon fresh dill, chopped
- 1 teaspoon ground black pepper
- 4 wontons wrap
- 1 egg white, whisked
- 1 teaspoon sesame oil

1. Chop the eggs and mix them up with cream cheese, dill, and ground black pepper.
2. Then place the egg mixture on the wonton wraps and roll them into the rolls.
3. Brush every roll with whisked egg white.
4. After this, preheat the air fryer to 395°F and brush the air fryer basket with sesame oil.
5. Arrange the egg rolls in the hot air fryer and cook them for 2 minutes from each side or until the rolls are golden brown.

Seed Porridge

Prep time: 10 minutes | Cook time: 12 minutes | Serves 3

- 1 tablespoon butter
- ¼ teaspoon nutmeg
- 1/3 cup heavy cream
- 1 egg
- ¼ teaspoon salt
- 3 tablespoons sesame seeds
- 3 tablespoons chia seeds

1. Place the butter in your air fryer basket tray.
2. Add the chia seeds, sesame seeds, heavy cream, nutmeg, and salt. Stir gently.
3. Beat the egg in a cup and whisk it with a fork.
4. Add the whisked egg to air fryer basket tray.
5. Stir the mixture with a wooden spatula.
6. Preheat your air fryer to 375°F.
7. Place the air fryer basket tray into air fryer and cook the porridge for 12-minutes.
8. Stir it about 3 times during the cooking process.
9. Remove the porridge from air fryer basket tray immediately and serve hot!

Peppers Bowls

Prep time: 5 minutes |Cook time: 20 minutes |Serves 4

- ½ cup cheddar cheese, shredded
- 2 tablespoons chives, chopped
- a pinch of salt and black pepper
- ¼ cup coconut cream
- 1 cup red bell peppers, chopped
- cooking spray

1. In a bowl, mix all the ingredients except the cooking spray and whisk well.
2. Pour the mix in a baking pan that fits the air fryer greased with cooking spray and place the pan in the machine.
3. Cook at 360 °F for 20 minutes, divide between plates and serve for breakfast.

Flax Meal Porridge

Prep time: 10 minutes | Cook time: 8 minutes |
Serves 4

- 2 tablespoons sesame seeds
- ½ teaspoon vanilla extract
- 1 tablespoon butter
- 1 tablespoon liquid stevia
- 3 tablespoons flax meal
- 1 cup almond milk
- 4 tablespoons chia seeds

1. Preheat your air fryer to 375°F. Put the sesame seeds, chia seeds, almond milk, flax meal, liquid Stevia and butter into the air fryer basket tray. Add the vanilla extract and cook porridge for 8-minutes.
2. When porridge is cooked stir it carefully then allow it to rest for 5-minutes before serving.

Breakfast Hash

Prep time: 5 minutes | Cook time: 8 minutes |
Serves 4

- 7-ounces bacon, cooked
- 1 zucchini, cubed into small pieces
- 4-ounces cheddar cheese, shredded
- 2 tablespoons butter
- 1 teaspoon ground thyme
- 1 teaspoon cilantro
- 1 teaspoon paprika
- 1 teaspoon ground black pepper
- 1 teaspoon salt

1. Chop the zucchini into small cubes and sprinkle with ground black pepper, salt, paprika, cilantro and ground thyme.
2. Preheat your air fryer to 400°F.
3. Add butter to the air fryer basket tray.
4. Melt the butter and add the zucchini cubes.
5. Cook the zucchini cubes for 5-minutes.

6. Meanwhile, shred the cheddar cheese.
7. Add the bacon to the zucchini cubes.
8. Sprinkle the zucchini mixture with shredded cheese and cook for 3-minutes more.
9. When cooking is completed, transfer the breakfast hash into serving bowls.

Herbed Breakfast Eggs

Prep time: 5 minutes | Cook time: 17 minutes |
Serves 2

- 4 eggs
- 1 teaspoon oregano
- 1 teaspoon parsley, dried
- ½ teaspoon sea salt
- 1 tablespoon chives, chopped
- 1 tablespoon cream
- 1 teaspoon paprika

1. Place the eggs in the air fryer basket and cook them for 17-minutes at 320°F.
2. Meanwhile, combine the parsley, oregano, cream, and salt in shallow bowl.
3. Chop the chives and add them to cream mixture.
4. When the eggs are cooked, place them in cold water and allow them to chill.
5. After this, peel the eggs and cut them into halves.
6. Remove the egg yolks and add yolks to cream mixture and mash to blend well with a fork.
7. Then fill the egg whites with the cream-egg yolk mixture. Serve immediately.

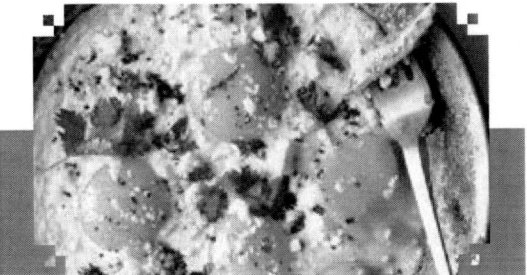

Breakfast Meatloaf Slices

Prep time: 10 minutes | Cook time: 20 minutes | Serves 6

- 8-ounces ground pork
- 7-ounces ground beef
- 1 teaspoon olive oil
- 1 teaspoon butter
- 1 tablespoon oregano, dried
- 1 teaspoon cayenne pepper
- 1 teaspoon salt
- 1 tablespoon chives
- 1 tablespoon almond flour
- 1 egg
- 1 onion, diced

1. Beat egg in a bowl.
2. Add the ground beef and ground pork.
3. Add the chives, almond flour, cayenne pepper, salt, dried oregano, and butter.
4. Add diced onion to ground beef mixture.
5. Use hands to shape a meatloaf mixture.
6. Preheat the air fryer to 350°F.
7. Spray the inside of the air fryer basket with olive oil and place the meatloaf inside it.
8. Cook the meatloaf for 20-minutes.
9. When the meatloaf has cooked, allow it to chill for a bit.
10. Slice and serve it.

Green Beans Salad

Prep time: 10 minutes | Cook time: 20 minutes | Serves 4

- 2 cups green beans, cut into medium pieces
- 2 cups fresh spinach, chopped
- 1 tablespoon avocado oil
- 1 tablespoons dried oregano
- 1 teaspoon coconut oil
- 1 teaspoon chili flakes

1. Mix green beans with dried oregano, coconut oil, and chili flakes.

2. Cook the green beans in the air fryer basket for 20 minutes at 365°F. Shake them from time to time.
3. Then mix cooked green beans with remaining ingredients and shake well.

Bacon Eggs

Prep time: 15 minutes |Cook time: 5 minutes |Serves 2

- 2 eggs, hard-boiled, peeled
- 4 bacon slices
- ½ teaspoon avocado oil
- 1 teaspoon mustard

1. Preheat the air fryer to 400°F. Then sprinkle the air fryer basket with avocado oil and place the bacon slices inside.
2. Flatten them in one layer and cook for 2 minutes from each side.
3. After this, cool the bacon to the room temperature. Wrap every egg into 2 bacon slices.
4. Secure the eggs with toothpicks and place them in the air fryer. Cook the wrapped eggs for 1 minute at 400°F.

Cheese Eggs and Leeks

Prep time: 5 minutes |Cook time: 7 minutes |Serves 2

- 2 leeks, chopped
- 4 eggs, whisked
- ¼ cup cheddar cheese, shredded
- ½ cup mozzarella cheese, shredded
- 1 teaspoon avocado oil

1. Preheat the air fryer to 400°F.
2. Then brush the air fryer basket with avocado oil and combine the eggs with the rest of the ingredients inside.
3. Cook for 7 minutes and serve.

Breakfast Liver Pate

Prep time: 5 minutes | Cook time: 10 minutes |
Serves 7

- 1 lb. chicken liver
- 1 teaspoon salt
- ½ teaspoon cilantro, dried
- 1 yellow onion, diced
- 1 teaspoon ground black pepper
- 1 cup water
- 4 tablespoons butter

1. Chop the chicken liver roughly and place it in the air fryer basket tray.
2. Add water to air fryer basket tray and add diced onion.
3. Preheat your air fryer to 360°F and cook chicken liver for 10-minutes.
4. When it is finished cooking, drain the chicken liver.
5. Transfer the chicken liver to blender, add butter, ground black pepper and dried cilantro and blend.
6. Once you get a pate texture, transfer to liver pate bowl and serve immediately or keep in the fridge for later.

Morning Time Sausages

Prep time: 10 minutes | Cook time: 12 minutes |
Serves 6

- 7-ounces ground chicken
- 7-ounces ground pork
- 1 teaspoon ground coriander
- 1 teaspoon basil, dried
- ½ teaspoon nutmeg
- 1 teaspoon olive oil
- 1 teaspoon minced garlic
- 1 tablespoon coconut flour
- 1 egg
- 1 teaspoon soy sauce
- 1 teaspoon sea salt
- ½ teaspoon ground black pepper

1. Combine the ground pork, chicken, soy sauce, ground black pepper, garlic, basil, coriander, nutmeg, sea salt, and egg. Add the coconut flour and mix the mixture well to combine. Preheat your air fryer to 360°F. Make medium-sized sausages with the ground meat mixture. Spray the inside of the air fryer basket tray with the olive oil.
2. Place prepared sausages into the air fryer basket and place inside of air fryer. Cook the sausages for 6-minutes. Turn the sausages over and cook for 6-minutes more.
3. When the cook time is completed, let the sausages chill for a little bit. Serve warm.

Eggs with Brussel Sprouts

Prep time: 5 minutes | Cook time: 20 minutes
|Serves 4

- 1-pound Brussel sprouts, shredded
- 8 eggs, beaten
- 1 teaspoon avocado oil
- 1 teaspoon ground turmeric
- ½ teaspoon salt

1. Mix all ingredients and stir until homogenous.
2. Pour the mixture in the air fryer basket and cook at 365°F for 20 minutes.

Minced Beef Keto Breakfast Sandwich

Prep time: 5 minutes | Cook time: 16 minutes | Serves 2

- 6-ounces minced beef
- 4 lettuce leaves
- 1 teaspoon flax seeds
- 1 teaspoon olive oil
- ½ teaspoon ground black pepper
- ½ teaspoon chili flakes
- ½ tomato, sliced
- ½ avocado, pitted, sliced

1. Combine the chili flakes with the minced beef and salt.
2. Add the flax seeds and stir the meat mixture using a fork.
3. Preheat your air fryer to 370°F.
4. Pour the olive oil into the air fryer basket tray.
5. Make 2 burgers from the beef mixture and place them in the air fryer basket.
6. Cook the burgers for 8-minutes on each side.
7. Meanwhile, slice the avocado and tomato.
8. Place the avocado and tomato onto 2 lettuce leaves.
9. Add the cooked minced beef burgers and serve them hot!

Paprika Zucchini Spread

Prep time:5 minutes |Cook time: 15 minutes |Serves 4

4 zucchinis, roughly chopped
1 tablespoon sweet paprika
Salt and black pepper to the taste
1 tablespoon butter, melted

1. Grease a baking pan that fits the Air Fryer with the butter, add all the ingredients, toss, and cook at 360 °F for 15 minutes.
2. Transfer to a blender, pulse well, divide into bowls and serve for breakfast.

No-Bun Breakfast Bacon Burger

Prep time: 10 minutes | Cook time: 8 minutes | Serves 2

- 8-ounces ground beef
- 2-ounces lettuce leaves
- ½ teaspoon minced garlic
- 1 teaspoon olive oil
- ½ teaspoon sea salt
- 1 teaspoon ground black pepper
- 1 teaspoon butter
- 4-ounces bacon, cooked
- 1 egg
- ½ yellow onion, diced
- ½ cucumber, slice finely
- ½ tomato, slice finely

1. Begin by whisking the egg in a bowl, then add the ground beef and combine well.
2. Add cooked, chopped bacon to the ground beef mixture.
3. Add butter, ground black pepper, minced garlic, and salt.
4. Mix and make burgers.
5. Preheat your air fryer to 370°F.
6. Spray the air fryer basket with olive oil and place the burgers inside of it.
7. Cook the burgers for 8-minutes on each side.
8. Meanwhile, slice the cucumber, onion, and tomato finely.
9. Place the tomato, onion, and cucumber onto the lettuce leaves.
10. When the burgers are cooked, allow them to chill at room temperature, and place them over the vegetables and serve.

Keto Spinach Quiche

Prep time: 10 minutes | Cook time: 21 minutes | Serves 6

- 6-ounces cheddar cheese, shredded
- 1 teaspoon olive oil
- 3 eggs
- 1 teaspoon ground black pepper
- ½ yellow onion, diced
- ¼ cup cream cheese
- 1 cup spinach
- 1 teaspoon sea salt
- 4 tablespoons water, boiled
- ½ cup almond flour

1. Combine the almond flour, water, and salt.
2. Mix and knead the dough.
3. Spray the inside of the fryer basket with olive oil.
4. Set your air fryer to 375°F.
5. Roll the dough and place it in your air fryer basket tray in the shape of the crust.
6. Place air fryer basket tray inside of air fryer and cook for 5-minutes.
7. Chop the spinach and combine it with the cream cheese and ground black pepper.
8. Dice the yellow onion and add it to the spinach mixture and stir.
9. Whisk eggs in a bowl.
10. When the quiche crust is cooked— transfer the spinach filling.
11. Sprinkle the filling top with shredded cheese and pour the whisked eggs over the top.
12. Set the air fryer to 350°F.
13. Cook the quiche for 7-minutes.
14. Reduce the heat to 300°F and cook the quiche for an additional 9-minutes.
15. Allow the quiche to chill thoroughly and then cut it into pieces for serving.

Bacon Bites

Prep time: 10 minutes | Cook time: 12 minutes |Serves 4

- 10 oz bacon, chopped
- 1 teaspoon dried dill
- 4 teaspoons cream cheese
- 1 teaspoon dried oregano

1. Put the bacon in the air fryer in one layer and bake for 12 minutes at 375°F. Shake the bacon from time to time to avoid burning.
2. Then mix bacon with remaining ingredients and make the balls (bites)

Scrambled Pancake Hash

Prep time: 10 minutes | Cook time: 9 minutes | Serves 7

- 1 egg
- ¼ cup heavy cream
- 5 tablespoons butter
- 1 cup coconut flour
- 1 teaspoon ground ginger
- 1 teaspoon salt
- 1 tablespoon apple cider vinegar
- 1 teaspoon baking soda

1. Combine the salt, baking soda, ground ginger and flour in a mixing bowl. In a separate bowl crack, the egg into it. Add butter and heavy cream. Mix well using a hand mixer. Combine the liquid and dry mixtures and stir until smooth.
2. Preheat your air fryer to 400°F. Pour the pancake mixture into the air fryer basket tray. Cook the pancake hash for 4-minutes. After this, scramble the pancake hash well and continue to cook for another 5-minutes more.
3. When dish is cooked, transfer it to serving plates, and serve hot!

Chapter 2

Poultry

Mediterranean-Style Chicken Fillets

Prep time: 15 minutes | Cook time:12 minutes |Serves 4

- 1 ½ pounds chicken fillets
- 1 tablespoon olive oil
- 1 teaspoon garlic, minced
- 1 tablespoon seasoning mix
- 1/2 teaspoon red pepper flakes, crushed
- Sea salt and ground black pepper, to taste

1. Pat the chicken dry with paper towels. Toss the chicken with the remaining ingredients.
2. Cook the chicken fillets at 380 °F for 12 minutes, turning them over halfway through the cooking time.
3. Bon appétit!

Lemon and Chili Chicken Drumsticks

Prep time:10 minutes |Cook time: 20 minutes |Serves 6

- 6 chicken drumsticks
- 1 teaspoon dried oregano
- 1 tablespoon lemon juice
- ½ teaspoon lemon zest, grated
- 1 teaspoon ground cumin
- ½ teaspoon chili flakes
- 1 teaspoon garlic powder
- ½ teaspoon ground coriander
- 1 tablespoon avocado oil

1. Rub the chicken drumsticks with dried oregano, lemon juice, lemon zest, ground cumin, chili flakes, garlic powder, and ground coriander.
2. Then sprinkle them with avocado oil and put in the air fryer.
3. Cook the chicken drumsticks for 20 minutes at 375°F.

Nutmeg Chicken Fillets

Prep time: 15 minutes | Cook time: 12 minutes |Serves 4

- 16 oz chicken fillets
- 1 teaspoon ground nutmeg
- 1 tablespoon avocado oil
- ½ teaspoon salt

1. Mix ground nutmeg with avocado oil and salt.
2. Then rub the chicken fillet with a nutmeg mixture and put it in the air fryer basket.
3. Cook the meal at 325°F for 12 minutes.

Cream Cheese Chicken Mix

Prep time:15 minutes |Cook time: 16 minutes |Serves 4

- 1-pound chicken wings
- ¼ cup cream cheese
- 1 tablespoon apple cider vinegar
- 1 teaspoon Truvia
- ½ teaspoon smoked paprika
- ½ teaspoon ground nutmeg
- 1 teaspoon avocado oil

1. In the mixing bowl mix up cream cheese, Truvia, apple cider vinegar, smoked paprika, and ground nutmeg.
2. Then add the chicken wings and coat them in the cream cheese mixture well.
3. Leave the chicken winds in the cream cheese mixture for 10-15 minutes to marinate.
4. Meanwhile, preheat the air fryer to 380°F.
5. Put the chicken wings in the air fryer and cook them for 8 minutes.
6. Then flip the chicken wings on another and brush with cream cheese marinade.
7. Cook the chicken wings for 8 minutes more.

Grilled Chicken with Garlic Sauce

Prep time: 5 minutes | Cook time: 15 minutes | Serves 4

- 1lb. chicken breast, cut into large cubes
- 2 bell peppers, chopped
- 1 zucchini
- 1 onion, chopped

For Garlic Sauce:
- 1 head garlic, peeled
- ¼ cup lemon juice
- 1 cup olive oil
- 1 teaspoon salt

Additional ingredients for the marinade:
- 1 teaspoon salt
- ½ cup olive oil

1. Soak 4 wooden skewers in water.
2. For your garlic sauce, place garlic cloves and salt into blender.
3. Then, add in about 1/8 of a cup of lemon juice and ½ a cup of olive oil.
4. Blend for about 10-seconds.
5. Keep half of the garlic sauce to serve with.
6. Take the other half of garlic sauce and add an additional ½ cup of olive oil and a teaspoon of salt and mix well—this will make your marinade.
7. Chop up the chicken, onion, bell peppers, and zucchini into 1-inch cubes or squares.
8. Mix them in a bowl with the marinade.
9. Place the cubes onto the skewers and cook them directly on the air fryer rack at 400°F for 15-minutes. Serve warm.

Apple Cider Vinegar Chicken Thighs

Prep time: 10 minutes | Cook time: 15 minutes | Serves 4

- 16 oz chicken thighs, skinless
- 1 teaspoon chili powder
- 1/3 cup apple cider vinegar
- 1 tablespoon avocado oil

1. Sprinkle the chicken thighs with chili powder, apple cider vinegar, and avocado oil.
2. Put them in the air fryer basket and cook at 380°F for 15 minutes.

Sweet and Sour Chicken Drumsticks

Prep time: 10 minutes | Cook time: 30 minutes | Serves 4

- 1 tablespoon keto tomato paste
- 2 tablespoons avocado oil
- 2 tablespoons coconut aminos
- 1 teaspoon garlic powder
- 1 teaspoon chili flakes
- 2-pounds chicken drumsticks
- 1 teaspoon Erythritol

1. Sprinkle the chicken drumsticks with tomato paste, avocado oil, coconut aminos, garlic powder, chili flakes, and Erythritol.
2. Put them in the air fryer and cook at 380°F for 15 minutes per side.

Turkey and Avocado Sliders

Prep time: 25 minutes | Cook time: 17 minutes |Serves 4

- 1 pound turkey, ground
- 1 tablespoon olive oil
- 1 avocado, peeled, pitted and chopped
- 2 garlic cloves, minced
- 1/2 cup breadcrumbs
- Kosher salt and ground black pepper, to taste
- 8 small rolls

1. Mix the turkey, olive oil, avocado, garlic, breadcrumbs, salt, and black pepper until everything is well combined. Form the mixture into eight small patties.
2. Cook the patties at 380 °F for about 20 minutes or until cooked through | make sure to turn them over halfway through the cooking time.
3. Serve your patties in the prepared rolls and enjoy!

Vinegar Chicken

Prep time: 20 minutes |Cook time: 15 minutes |Serves4

- 16 oz chicken thighs, skinless
- 1 teaspoon ground celery root
- 1 teaspoon dried celery leaves
- 1 teaspoon apple cider vinegar
- ½ teaspoon salt
- 1 tablespoon sunflower oil

1. Rub the chicken thighs with the celery root, dried celery leaves, and salt. Then sprinkle the chicken with apple cider vinegar and sunflower oil.
2. Leave it for 15 minutes to marinate. After this, preheat the air fryer to 325°F.
3. Put the chicken thighs in the air fryer and cook them for 12 minutes. Then flip the chicken on another side and cook

for 3 minutes more.
4. Transfer the cooked chicken thighs on the plate.

Chicken Salad Sandwich

Prep time: 20 minutes | Cook time:12 minutes |Serves 4

- 1 pound chicken breasts, boneless and skinless
- 1 stalks celery, chopped
- 1 carrot, chopped
- 1 small onion, chopped
- 1 cup mayonnaise
- Sea salt and ground black pepper, to taste
- 4 sandwich buns

1. Pat the chicken dry with paper towels. Place the chicken in a lightly oiled cooking basket.
2. Cook the chicken breasts at 380 °F for 12 minutes, turning them over halfway through the cooking time.
3. Shred the chicken breasts using two forks and transfer it to a salad bowl and add in the celery, carrot, onion, mayo, salt, and pepper.
4. Toss to combine and serve in sandwich buns. Enjoy!

Spinach and Feta Stuffed Chicken

Prep time: 25 minutes | Cook time:20 minutes |Serves 4

- 1 pound chicken breasts, skinless, boneless and cut into pieces
- 2 tablespoons olives, chopped
- 1 garlic clove, minced
- 2 cups spinach, torn into pieces
- 2 ounces feta cheese
- Sea salt and ground black pepper, to taste
- 2 tablespoons olive oil

1. Flatten the chicken breasts with a mallet.
2. Stuff each piece of chicken with olives, garlic, spinach, and cheese. Roll them up and secure with toothpicks.
3. Sprinkle the chicken with the salt, black pepper, and olive oil.
4. Place the stuffed chicken breasts in the Air Fryer cooking basket. Cook the chicken at 400 °F for about 20 minutes, turning them over halfway through the cooking time.
5. Bon appétit!

Rosemary Citrus Chicken

Prep time: 5 minutes | Cook time 15 minutes | Serves 2

- 1 lb. chicken thighs
- 1/2 teaspoon rosemary, fresh, chopped
- 1/8 teaspoon thyme, dried
- ½ cup tangerine juice
- 2 tablespoons white wine
- 1 teaspoon garlic, minced
- salt and pepper to taste
- 2 tablespoons lemon juice

1. Place the chicken thighs in a mixing bowl. In another bowl, mix tangerine juice, garlic, white wine, lemon juice, rosemary, pepper, salt, and thyme.
2. Pour the mixture over chicken thighs and place in the fridge for 20-minutes. Preheat your air fryer to 350°F and place your marinated chicken in air fryer basket and cook for 15-minutes. Serve hot and enjoy!

BBQ Wings

Prep time: 10 minutes | Cook time: 18 minutes |Serves 4

- 2-pound chicken wings
- 1 cup keto BBQ sauce
- 1 teaspoon olive oil

1. Mix BBQ sauce with olive oil.
2. Brush the chicken wings carefully with the BQ sauce mixture and put it in the air fryer.
3. Cook the chicken wings for 9 minutes per side at 375°F.

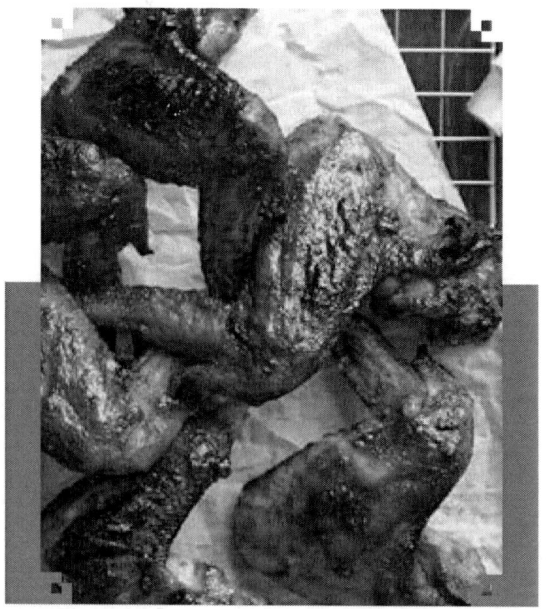

Stuffed Garlic Chicken

Prep time: 5 minutes | Cook time 15 minutes | Serves 2

- ¼ cup of tomatoes, sliced
- ½ tablespoon garlic, minced
- 2 basil leaves
- salsa for serving
- 1 prosciutto slice
- 2 teaspoons parmesan cheese, freshly grated
- 2 boneless chicken breasts
- pepper and salt to taste

1. Cut the side of the chicken breast to make a pocket. Stuff each pocket with tomato slices, garlic, grated cheese and basil leaves. Cut a slice of prosciutto in half to form 2 equal size pieces.
2. Season chicken with salt and pepper and wrap each with a slice of prosciutto. Preheat your air fryer to 325°F. Place the stuffed chicken breasts into air fryer basket and cook for 15-minutes. Serve chicken breasts with salsa.

Asparagus Chicken

Prep time: 15 minutes | Cook time: 25 minutes |Serves 4

- 1 cup asparagus, chopped
- 1-pound chicken thighs, skinless, boneless
- 1 teaspoon onion powder
- 1 oz scallions, chopped
- 1 tablespoon coconut oil, melted
- 1 teaspoon smoked paprika

1. Mix chicken thighs with onion powder, coconut oil, and smoked paprika.
2. Put the chicken thighs in the air fryer and cook at 325°F for 20 minutes.
3. Then flip the chicken thighs on another side and top with chopped asparagus and scallions.
4. Cook the meal for 5 minutes more.

Cinnamon Chicken Thighs

Prep time: 5 minutes |Cook time: 30 minutes |Serves 4

- 2 pounds chicken thighs
- a pinch of salt and black pepper
- 2 tablespoons olive oil
- ½ teaspoon cinnamon, ground

1. Season the chicken thighs with salt and pepper, and rub with the rest of the ingredients.
2. Put the chicken thighs in air fryer's basket, cook at 360 °F for 15 minutes on each side, divide between plates and serve.

Buttery Chicken Wings

Prep time: 5 minutes |Cook time: 30 minutes |Serves 4

- 2 pounds chicken wings
- salt and black pepper to the taste
- 3 garlic cloves, minced
- 3 tablespoons butter, melted
- ½ cup heavy cream
- ½ teaspoon basil, dried
- ½ teaspoon oregano, dried
- ¼ cup parmesan, grated

1. In a baking dish that fits your air fryer, mix the chicken wings with all the ingredients except the parmesan and toss.
2. Put the dish to your air fryer and cook at 380 °F for 30 minutes.
3. Sprinkle the cheese on top, leave the mix aside for 10 minutes, divide between plates and serve.

Sriracha Herb Turkey

Prep time: 1 hour and 5 minutes | Cook time:60 minutes |Serves 5

- 2 pounds turkey breasts, rib bones trimmed
- 4 tablespoons butter, melted
- 1 teaspoon Sriracha sauce
- 1 tablespoon fresh cilantro, chopped
- 1 tablespoon fresh parsley, chopped
- 1 tablespoon fresh thyme, chopped
- Kosher salt and freshly ground black pepper, to taste

1. Pat the turkey breasts dry with paper towels. Toss the turkey breasts with the remaining ingredients.
2. Cook the turkey breasts at 350 °F for 1 hour, turning them over every 20 minutes.
3. Bon appétit!

Garlic Chicken Wings

Prep time:5 minutes |Cook time: 30 minutes |Serves 4

- 2 pounds chicken wings
- ¼ cup olive oil
- Juice of 2 lemons
- Zest of 1 lemon, grated Apinch of salt and black pepper
- 2 garlic cloves, minced

1. In a bowl, mix the chicken wings with the rest of the ingredients and toss well.
2. Put the chicken wings in your air fryer's basket and cook at 400 °F for 30 minutes, shaking halfway.
3. Divide between plates and serve with a side salad.

Chili and Paprika Chicken Wings

Prep time: 10 minutes |Cook time: 12 minutes |Serves5

- 1-pound chicken wings
- 1 teaspoon ground paprika
- 1 teaspoon chili powder
- ½ teaspoon salt
- 1 tablespoon sunflower oil

1. Pour the sunflower oil in the shallow bowl. Add chili powder and ground paprika.
2. Gently stir the mixture. Sprinkle the chicken wings with red chili mixture and salt.
3. Preheat the air fryer to 400°F. Place the chicken wings in the preheated air fryer in one layer and cook for 6 minutes.
4. Then flip the wings on another side and cook for 6 minutes more.

Mexican Chicken Taquitos

Prep time: 20 minutes | Cook time:12 minutes |Serves 5

- 3/4 pound chicken breasts, boneless and skinless
- Kosher salt and ground black pepper, to taste
- 1/2 teaspoon red chili powder
- 5 small corn tortillas
- 5 ounces Cotija cheese, crumbled

1. Pat the chicken dry with kitchen towels. Toss the chicken breasts with the salt, pepper, and red chili powder.
2. Cook the chicken at 380 °F for 12 minutes, turning them over halfway through the cooking time.
3. Place the shredded chicken and cheese on one end of each tortilla. Roll them up tightly and transfer them to a lightly oiled Air Fryer basket.
4. Bake your taquitos at 360 °F for 6 minutes. Bon appétit!

Ranch Chicken Drumsticks

Prep time: 25 minutes | Cook time:20 minutes
|Serves 4

- 1/2 cup all-purpose flour
- 1 tablespoon Ranch seasoning mix
- 1 pound chicken drumsticks
- 1 tablespoon hot sauce
- Sea salt and ground black pepper, to taste

1. Pat the chicken drumsticks dry with paper towels. Toss the chicken drumsticks with the remaining ingredients.
2. Cook the chicken drumsticks at 370 °F for 20 minutes, turning them over halfway through the cooking time.
3. Bon appétit!

Sicilian Chicken Fillets

Prep time: 20 minutes | Cook time:12 minutes
|Serves 4

- 1 ½ pounds chicken fillets
- 2 tablespoons olive oil
- 1 teaspoon smoked paprika
- 1 teaspoon Italian seasoning mix
- Sea salt and ground black pepper, to taste
- 1/2 cup Pecorino Romano cheese, grated

1. Pat the chicken fillets dry with paper towels. Toss the chicken fillets with the olive oil and spices.
2. Cook the chicken fillets at 380 °F for 12 minutes, turning them over halfway through the cooking time.
3. Top the chicken fillets with grated cheese and serve warm. Bon appétit!

Authentic Chicken Fajitas

Prep time: 35 minutes | Cook time:15 minutes
|Serves 4

- 1 pound chicken legs, boneless, skinless, cut into pieces
- 2 tablespoons canola oil
- 1 red bell pepper, sliced
- 1 yellow bell pepper, sliced
- 1 jalapeno pepper, sliced
- 1 onion, sliced
- 1/2 teaspoon onion powder
- 1/2 teaspoon garlic powder
- Sea salt and ground black pepper, to taste

1. Pat the chicken dry with paper towels. Toss the chicken legs with 1 tablespoon of the canola oil.
2. Cook the chicken at 380 °F for 15 minutes, shaking the basket halfway through the cooking time.
3. Add the remaining ingredients to the Air Fryer basket and turn the heat to 400 °F. Let it cook for 15 minutes more or until cooked through.
4. Bon appétit!

Chapter 3

Beef, Pork and Lamb

Thyme Pork Sausages

Prep time: 10 minutes | Cook time: 25 minutes |Serves 4

- 2-pounds pork sausages
- 1 tablespoon dried thyme
- 1 teaspoon olive oil
- 1 teaspoon salt

1. Sprinkle the pork sausages with dried thyme, olive oil, and salt.
2. Put the pork sausages in the air fryer.
3. Cook the meal at 375°F for 25 minutes. Flip the pork sausages after 15 minutes of cooking.

Mexican-Style Pork Tacos

Prep time: 1 hour | Cook time:55 minutes |Serves 4

- 2 ancho chiles, seeded and minced
- 2 garlic cloves, chopped
- 1 tablespoon olive oil
- Kosher salt and freshly ground black pepper, to season
- 1 teaspoon dried Mexican oregano
- 1 ½ pounds pork butt
- 4 corn tortillas, warmed

1. Toss all ingredients, except for the tortillas, in a lightly greased Air Fryer cooking basket.
2. Air fry the pork butt at 360 °F for 55 minutes, turning it over halfway through the cooking time.
3. Using two forks, shred the pork and serve in tortillas with toppings of choice. Serve immediately!

Cream Cheese Pork

Prep time: 15 minutes |Cook time: 20 minutes |Serves 4

- 16 oz pork tenderloin
- 1 teaspoon liquid smoke

- 1 teaspoon mustard
- 1 teaspoon cream cheese
- ½ teaspoon ground paprika
- 1 teaspoon avocado oil

1. In the mixing bowl mix up liquid smoked, mustard, cream cheese, and ground paprika. Add avocado oil and. Stir the mixture.
2. Then rub the pork tenderloin with the smoky mixture and wrap in the foil.
3. Preheat the air fryer to 375°F. Put the wrapped tenderloin in the air fryer basket and cook it for 20 minutes.
4. Then discard the foil and slice the tenderloin into the servings.

Lamb Burgers

Prep time: 15 minutes |Cook time: 16 minutes |Serves 2

- 8 oz lamb, minced
- ½ teaspoon salt
- ½ teaspoon ground black pepper
- ½ teaspoon dried cilantro
- 1 tablespoon water
- cooking spray

1. In the mixing bowl mix up minced lamb, salt, ground black pepper, dried cilantro, and water.
2. Stir the meat mixture carefully with the help of the spoon and make 2 burgers. Preheat the air fryer to 375°F.
3. Spray the air fryer basket with cooking spray and put the burgers inside.
4. Cook them for 8 minutes from each side.

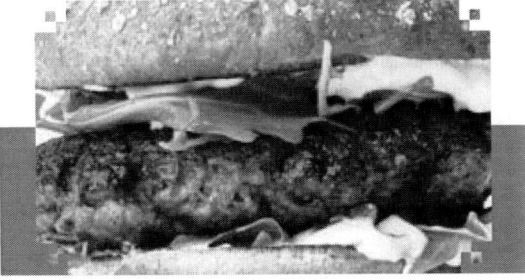

Smoked Pork

Prep time: 20 minutes |Cook time: 20 minutes |Serves 5

- 1-pound pork shoulder
- 1 tablespoon liquid smoke
- 1 tablespoon olive oil
- 1 teaspoon salt

1. Mix up liquid smoke, salt, and olive oil in the shallow bowl.
2. Then carefully brush the pork shoulder with the liquid smoke mixture from each side.
3. Make the small cuts in the meat. Preheat the air fryer to 390°F. Put the pork shoulder in the air fryer basket and cook the meat for 10 minutes.
4. After this, flip the meat on another side and cook it for 10 minutes more. Let the cooked pork shoulder rest for 10-15 minutes. Shred it with the help of 2 forks.

Pork Skewers

Prep time: 20 minutes | Cook time: 20 minutes |Serves 4

- 1-pound pork loin, chopped
- 1 tablespoon avocado oil
- 3 tablespoons apple cider vinegar
- 1 teaspoon coconut cream
- 1 teaspoon ground black pepper
- ½ teaspoon salt

1. In the shallow bowl, mix avocado oil with apple cider vinegar, coconut cream, ground black pepper, and salt.
2. Then mix pork loin with avocado oil mixture and leave for 10 minutes to marinate.
3. Sting the meat into skewers and put in the air fryer.
4. Cook them at 400°F for 20 minutes. Flip the skewers from time to time.

Bacon-Wrapped Stuffed Zucchini Boats

Prep time: 10 minutes | Cook time: 15 minutes | Serves 4

- ½ a teaspoon of fresh ground black pepper
- 1 teaspoon sea salt
- 5-ounces cream cheese
- 8-mushrooms, finely chopped
- 1 tablespoon Italian parsley, chopped
- 1 tablespoon finely chopped dill
- 3 garlic cloves, peeled, pressed
- 1 sweet red pepper, finely chopped
- 2 large zucchinis
- 12 bacon strips
- 1 medium onion, chopped

1. Preheat your air fryer to 350°F.
2. Trim the ends off zucchini.
3. Cut zucchini in half length-wise.
4. Scoop out pulp, leaving ¼-inch thick shells.
5. Stir pulp in mixing bowl.
6. Add onion, garlic, herbs, pepper, cream cheese, salt, and pepper.
7. Mix well to combine.
8. Fill individual shells with the same amount of stuffing.
9. Wrap three bacon strips around each zucchini boat such that the ends end up underneath.
10. Place them directly on the air fryer rack and bake turning the temperature up to 375°F for 15-minutes. Remove and serve immediately.

Air Fried Pork Apple Balls

Prep time: 5 minutes | Cook time 15 minutes | Serves 8

- 2 cups pork, minced
- 6 basil leaves, chopped
- 2 tablespoons cheddar cheese, grated
- 4 garlic cloves, minced
- ½ cup apple, peeled, cored, chopped
- 1 large white onion, diced
- salt and pepper to taste
- 2 teaspoons dijon mustard
- 1 teaspoon liquid stevia

1. Add pork minced in a bowl then add diced onion and apple into a bowl and mix well. Add the stevia, mustard, garlic, cheese, basil, salt and pepper and combine well.
2. Make small round balls from the mixture and place them into air fryer basket. Cook at 350°F for 15-minutes. Serve and enjoy!

Beef with Tomato Sauce and Fennel

Prep time:5 minutes |Cook time: 20 minutes |Serves 4

- 2 tablespoons olive oil
- 1 pound beef, cut into strips
- 1 fennel bulb, sliced
- Salt and black pepper to the taste
- 1 teaspoon sweet paprika
- ¼ cup keto tomato sauce

1. Heat up a pan that fits the air fryer with the oil over medium-high heat, add the beef and brown for 5 minutes.
2. Add the rest of the ingredients, toss, put the pan in the machine and cook at 380 °F for 15 minutes.
3. Divide the mix between plates and serve.

Mustard Pork

Prep time:5 minutes |Cook time: 30 minutes |Serves 4

- 1 pound pork tenderloin, trimmed
- A pinch of salt and black pepper
- 2 tablespoons olive oil
- 3 tablespoons mustard
- 2 tablespoons balsamic vinegar

1. In a bowl, mix the pork tenderloin with the rest of the ingredients and rub well.
2. Put the roast in your air fryer's basket and cook at 380 °F for 30 minutes.
3. Slice the roast, divide between plates and serve.

Lemon Pork Belly

Prep time: 15 minutes | Cook time: 55 minutes | Serves 6

- 1-pound pork belly
- 1 teaspoon lemon zest, grated
- 2 tablespoons lemon juice
- ½ teaspoon salt
- ½ teaspoon chili powder

1. Rub the pork belly with lemon zest, lemon juice, salt, and chili powder.
2. Put it in the air fryer and cook at 350°F for 55 minutes.

Keto Onion Pork Cubes

Prep time: 5 minutes | Cook time: 18 minutes | Serves 4

- 1 pound pork stew meat, cubed
- 1 teaspoon onion powder
- 1 oz scallions, chopped
- 1 tablespoon olive oil
- ½ teaspoon white pepper
- ½ teaspoon salt

1. Put all ingredients in the air fryer and gently mix.
2. Cook the pork cubes at 380°F for 9 minutes per side,

Dad's Spicy Burgers

Prep time: 20 minutes | Cook time:15 minutes |Serves 3

- 3/4 pound beef
- 2 tablespoons onion, minced
- 1 teaspoon garlic, minced
- 1 teaspoon cayenne pepper
- Sea salt and ground black pepper, to taste
- 1 teaspoon red chili powder
- 3 hamburger buns

1. Mix the beef, onion, garlic, cayenne pepper, salt, black pepper, and red chili powder until everything is well combined. Form the mixture into three patties.
2. Cook the burgers at 380 °F for about 15 minutes or until cooked through, make sure to turn them over halfway through the cooking time.
3. Serve your burgers on the prepared buns and enjoy!

Lemon Pork

Prep time:15 minutes |Cook time: 25 minutes |Serves 4

- 4 pork chops
- 2 tablespoons olive oil Apinch of salt and black pepper
- 2 garlic cloves, minced
- 4 teaspoons mustard
- 2 teaspoons lemon zest, grated
- Juice of 1 lemon

1. In a bowl, mix the pork chops with the other ingredients, toss and keep in the fridge for 15 minutes Put the pork chops in your air fryer's basket and cook at 390 °F for 25 minutes.
2. Divide between plates and serve with a side salad.

Ground Pork Dinner Rolls

Prep time: 20 minutes | Cook time:415minutes |Serves 4

- 1 pound ground pork
- Sea salt and freshly ground black pepper, to taste
- 1 teaspoon red pepper flakes, crushed
- 1/2 cup scallions, chopped
- 2 garlic cloves, minced
- 1 tablespoon olive oil
- 1 tablespoon soy sauce
- 8 dinner rolls, split

1. In a mixing bowl, thoroughly combine the pork, spices, scallions, garlic, olive oil, and soy sauce. Form the mixture into four patties.
2. Cook the patties at 380 °F for about 15 minutes or until cooked through, make sure to turn them over halfway through the cooking time.
3. Serve the patties in dinner rolls and enjoy!

Lime Lamb Curry

Prep time: 5 minutes |Cook time: 35 minutes |Serves 4

- 2 tablespoons olive oil
- 1 and ½ pounds lamb meat, cubed
- A pinch of salt and black pepper
- 15 ounces tomatoes, chopped
- Juice of 2 limes
- 1 teaspoon sweet paprika
- 1 cup beef stock
- 1-inch ginger, grated
- 2 hot chilies, chopped
- 2 red bell peppers, chopped
- 4 garlic cloves, minced
- 2 teaspoons turmeric powder
- 1 tablespoon green curry paste

1. Heat up a pan that fits your air fryer with the oil over medium heat, add the meat and brown for 5 minutes.
2. Add the rest of the ingredients, toss, put the pan in the fryer and cook at 380 °F for 30 minutes. Divide everything into bowls and serve.

Creamy Pork Mix

Prep time: 5 minutes |Cook time: 25 minutes |Serves 4

- 1 pound pork stew meat, cubed
- 4 teaspoons sweet paprika
- A pinch of salt and black pepper
- 1 cup coconut cream
- 1 tablespoon butter, melted
- 1 tablespoon parsley, chopped

1. Heat up a pan that fits the air fryer with the butter over medium heat, add the meat and brown for 5 minutes.
2. Add the remaining ingredients, toss, put the pan in the air fryer, cook at 390 °F for 20 minutes more, divide into bowls and serve.

Oregano Pork Chops

Prep time: 10 minutes | Cook time: 18 minutes |Serves 4

- 4 pork chops
- 1 tablespoon dried oregano
- ½ teaspoon minced garlic
- 2 tablespoons olive oil

1. Heat the pan well and put the pork chops inside.
2. Roast them for 2 minutes per side and transfer in the air fryer.
3. Sprinkle the meat with dried oregano and minced garlic.
4. Cook the pork chops at 365°F for 7 minutes per side.

Wrapped Pork Tenderloin

Prep time: 15 minutes | Cook time: 16 minutes |Serves 2

- 12 oz pork tenderloin
- 2 oz bacon, sliced
- 1 teaspoon ground paprika
- ½ teaspoon chili powder

1. Rub the pork tenderloin with ground paprika and chili powder.
2. Then wrap the meat in the bacon and put in the air fryer.
3. Cook the meat at 375°F for 8 minutes per side.

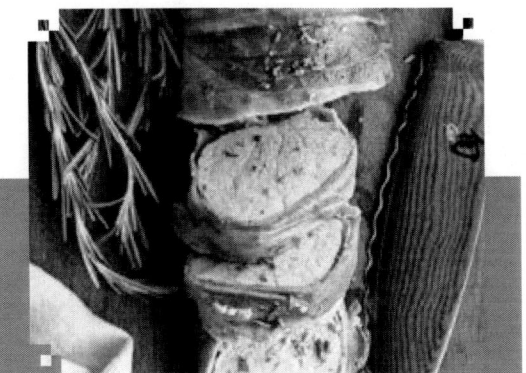

Cinnamon Pork Chops

Prep time: 10 minutes | Cook time: 20 minutes |Serves 4

- 4 pork chops
- 1 teaspoon ground cinnamon
- 1 teaspoon olive oil
- ½ teaspoon salt

1. Rub the pork chops with ground cinnamon, olive oil, and salt.
2. Put the pork chops in the air fryer and cook them for 8-9 minutes per side at 375°F.

Cajun Pork and Peppers Mix

Prep time: 5 minutes |Cook time: 35 minutes |Serves 2

- 1 pound pork stew meat, cut into strips
- 1 tablespoon cajun seasoning
- 2 red bell peppers, sliced
- 1 pound tomatoes, chopped
- 4 garlic cloves, minced
- 2 tablespoons coconut oil, melted
- a pinch of salt and black pepper

1. Heat up a pan that fits the air fryer with the oil over medium-high heat, add the pork meat, seasoning, garlic, salt and pepper, toss and brown for 5 minutes.
2. Add the remaining ingredients, toss, put the pan in the fryer and cook at 390 °F for 30 minutes. Divide everything between plates and serve.

Chives Beef

Prep time:25 minutes |Cook time: 10 minutes |Serves 2

- 10 oz steak
- 2 tablespoons coconut flour
- 1 teaspoon sunflower oil
- ½ teaspoon garlic powder
- 2 tablespoons apple cider vinegar
- 1 teaspoon coconut aminos
- 4 tablespoons water
- 1 tablespoon Erythritol
- 1 teaspoon chives, chopped

1. Slice the steak into the long thin strips and sprinkle with coconut flour. Shake the meat gently.
2. Preheat the air fryer to 395°F.
3. Put the sliced flank steak in the air fryer and cook it for 5 minutes from each side.
4. Meanwhile, pour sunflower oil in the saucepan.
5. Add garlic powder, apple cider vinegar, soy sauce, water, and Erythritol.
6. Bring the liquid to boil and remove from the heat.
7. When the meat is cooked, put it in the hot sauce and mix up well.
8. Leave the meat to soak in the sauce for 5-10 minutes.

Coated Pork Chops

Prep time: 15 minutes | Cook time: 16 minutes |Serves 4

- 4 pork chops
- 1 egg, beaten
- 3 tablespoons coconut shred
- 1 teaspoon salt
- Cooking spray

1. Sprinkle the pork chops with salt and dip in the egg.
2. Then coat the pork chops in the coconut shred and put in the air fryer.
3. Spray the pork chops with cooking spray and cook them at 375°F for 8 minutes.

Lamb Sausages

Prep time: 25 minutes |Cook time: 10 minutes |Serves 4

- 4 sausage links
- 12 oz ground lamb
- 1 teaspoon minced garlic
- ½ teaspoon onion powder
- 1 teaspoon dried parsley
- ½ teaspoon salt
- 1 teaspoon ghee
- ½ teaspoon ground ginger
- 1 tablespoon sesame oil

1. In the mixing bowl mix up ground lamb, minced garlic, onion powder, dried parsley, salt, and ground ginger.
2. Then fill the sausage links with the ground lamb mixture. Secure the ends of the sausages.
3. Brush the air fryer basket with sesame oil from inside and put the sausages.
4. Then sprinkle the sausages with ghee. Cook the lamb sausages for 10 minutes at 400°F.
5. Flip them on another side after 5 minutes of cooking.

Garlic Pork and Bok Choy

Prep time: 5 minutes |Cook time: 35 minutes |Serves 4

- 4 pork chops, boneless
- 1 bok choy head, torn
- 2 cups chicken stock
- 2 tablespoons coconut aminos
- 2 garlic cloves, minced
- a pinch of salt and black pepper
- 2 tablespoons coconut oil, melted

1. Heat up a pan that fits the air fryer with the oil over medium-high heat, add the pork chops and brown for 5 minutes.

2. Add the garlic, salt and pepper and cook for another minute. Add the rest of the ingredients except the bok choy and cook at 380 °F for 25 minutes.
3. Add the bok choy, cook for 5 minutes more, divide everything between plates and serve.

Mushroom and Beef Patties

Prep time: 15 minutes | Cook time:15 minutes |Serves 4

- 1 pound ground chuck
- 2 garlic cloves, minced
- 1 small onion, chopped
- 1 cup mushrooms, chopped
- 1 teaspoon cayenne pepper
- Sea salt and ground black pepper, to taste
- 4 brioche rolls

1. Mix the ground chuck, garlic, onion, mushrooms, cayenne pepper, salt, and black pepper until everything is well combined. Form the mixture into four patties.
2. Cook the patties at 380 °F for about 15 minutes or until cooked through, make sure to turn them over halfway through the cooking time.
3. Serve your patties on the prepared brioche rolls and enjoy!

Hot Sriracha Burgers

Prep time: 20 minutes | Cook time:15 minutes
|Serves 5

- 1 pound pork
- 1/2 pound beef
- 1/2 cup scallions, chopped
- 1 teaspoon garlic, minced
- 1 tablespoon Sriracha sauce
- 5 tablespoons tortilla chips, crushed
- 2 tablespoons olive oil
- Sea salt and ground black pepper, to taste
- 5 ciabatta rolls

1. In a mixing bowl, thoroughly combine the meat, scallions, garlic, Sriracha sauce, tortilla chips, olive oil, salt, and black pepper. Form the mixture into four patties.
2. Cook the burgers at 380 °F for about 15 minutes or until cooked through, make sure to turn them over halfway through the cooking time.
3. Serve your burgers with ciabatta rolls.

Bon appétit!

Old-Fashioned Meatloaf

Prep time: 30 minutes | Cook time:25 minutes
|Serves 4

- 1 ½ pounds ground chuck
- 1 egg, beaten
- 2 tablespoons olive oil
- 4 tablespoons crackers, crushed
- 1/2 cup shallots, minced
- 2 garlic cloves, minced
- 1 tablespoon fresh rosemary, chopped
- 1 tablespoon fresh thyme, chopped
- Sea salt and ground black pepper, to taste

1. Thoroughly combine all ingredients until everything is well combined.
2. Scrape the beef mixture into a lightly oiled baking pan and transfer it to the Air Fryer cooking basket.
3. Cook your meatloaf at 390 °F for 25 minutes. Bon appétit!

Chapter 4

Fish & Seafood

Mom's Famous Fish Sticks

Prep time: 15 minutes | Cook time:10 minutes |Serves 4

- 1/2 cup all-purpose flour
- 1 large egg
- 2 tablespoons buttermilk
- 1/2 cup crackers, crushed
- 1 teaspoon garlic powder
- Sea salt and ground black pepper, to taste
- 1/2 teaspoon cayenne pepper
- 1 pound tilapia fillets, cut into strips

1. In a shallow bowl, place the flour. Whisk the egg and buttermilk in a second bowl, and mix the crushed crackers and spices in a third bowl.
2. Dip the fish strips in the flour mixture, then in the whisked eggs | finally, roll the fish strips over the cracker mixture until they are well coated on all sides.
3. Arrange the fish sticks in the Air Fryer basket.
4. Cook the fish sticks at 400 °F for about 10 minutes, shaking the basket halfway through the cooking time.
5. Bon appétit!

Chili and Paprika Squid

Prep time: 10 minutes | Cook time:5minutes |Serves 5

- 1 ½ pounds squid, cut into pieces
- 1 chili pepper, chopped
- 1 small lemon, squeezed
- 2 tablespoons olive oil
- 1 tablespoon capers, drained
- 2 garlic cloves, minced
- 1 tablespoon coriander, chopped
- 2 tablespoons parsley, chopped
- 1 teaspoon sweet paprika
- Sea salt and ground black pepper, to taste

1. Toss all ingredients in a lightly greased Air Fryer cooking basket.
2. Cook your squid at 400 °F for 5 minutes, tossing the basket halfway through the cooking time.
3. Bon appétit!

Lemon Shrimp and Zucchinis

Prep time: 5 minutes |Cook time: 15 minutes |Serves 4

- 1 pound shrimp, peeled and deveined
- a pinch of salt and black pepper
- 2 zucchinis, cut into medium cubes
- 1 tablespoon lemon juice
- 1 tablespoon olive oil
- 1 tablespoon garlic, minced

1. In a pan that fits the air fryer, combine all the ingredients, toss, put the pan in the machine and cook at 370 °F for 15 minutes.
2. Divide between plates and serve right away.

Turmeric Cod

Prep time: 10 minutes | Cook time: 7 minutes | Serves 2

- 12 oz cod fillet
- 1 teaspoon ground turmeric
- 1 teaspoon chili flakes
- 1 tablespoon coconut oil, melted
- ½ teaspoon salt

1. Mix coconut oil with ground turmeric, chili flakes, and salt.
2. Then mix cod fillet with ground turmeric and put in the air fryer basket.
3. Cook the cod at 325°F for 7 minutes.

Turmeric Fish Fingers

Prep time: 15 minutes |Cook time: 9 minutes |Serves4

- 1-pound cod fillet
- ½ cup almond flour
- 2 eggs, beaten
- ½ teaspoon ground turmeric
- 1 tablespoon flax meal
- 1 teaspoon salt
- 1 teaspoon avocado oil

1. Slice the cod fillets into the strips (fingers). In the mixing bowl, mix up eggs, ground turmeric, and salt. Stir the liquid until salt is dissolved.
2. Then in the separated bowl mix up almond flour and flax meal.
3. Dip the cod fingers in the egg mixture and coat in the almond flour mixture. Preheat the air fryer to 400°F.
4. Place the fish fingers in the air fryer basket in one layer and sprinkle with avocado oil.
5. Cook the fish fingers for 4 minutes. Then flip them on another side and cook for 5 minutes more or until the fish fingers are golden brown.

Fish with Capers & Herb Sauce

Prep time: 10 minutes | Cook time: 15 minutes | Serves 4

- 2 cod fillets
- ¼ cup almond flour
- 1 teaspoon dijon mustard
- 1 egg

Sauce:
- 2 tablespoons of light sour cream
- 2 teaspoons capers
- 1 tablespoon tarragon, chopped
- 1 tablespoon fresh dill, chopped
- 2 tablespoons red onion, chopped
- 2 tablespoons dill pickle, chopped

1. Add all of the sauce ingredients into a small mixing bowl and mix until well blended then place in the fridge. In a bowl mix Dijon mustard and egg and sprinkle the flour over a plate.
2. Dip the cod fillets first into the egg and coat, then dip them into the flour, coating them on both sides. Preheat your air fryer to 300°F, place fillets into air fryer and cook for 10-minutes.
3. Place fillets on serving dishes and drizzle with sauce and serve.

Mustard Tilapia

Prep time: 10 minutes | Cook time: 14 minutes | Serves 4

- 1 cup Monterey Jack cheese, grated
- 4 tilapia fillets
- ¼ teaspoon ground cumin
- 1 tablespoon Dijon mustard

1. Rub the tilapia fillets with ground cumin and Dijon mustard.
2. Put the fish in the air fryer in one layer and top with cheese.
3. Cook the tilapia for 14 minutes at 370°F.

Fried Crawfish

Prep time:10 minutes |Cook time: 5 minutes |Serves 4

- 1-pound crawfish
- 1 tablespoon avocado oil
- 1 teaspoon onion powder
- 1 tablespoon rosemary, chopped

1. Preheat the air fryer to 340°F.
2. Place the crawfish in the air fryer basket and sprinkle with avocado oil and rosemary.
3. Add the onion powder and stir the crawfish gently.
4. Cook the meal for 5 minutes.

Air Fried Spinach Fish

Prep time: 5 minutes | Cook time: 12 minutes | Serves 2

- 4-ounces of spinach leaves
- 1 large egg, beaten
- 2 tablespoons olive oil
- 2 cups almond flour
- 2 white fish fillets
- Pinch of sea salt
- Black pepper to taste

1. In a deep bowl, place the beaten egg, almond flour, sea salt, black pepper, and spinach leaves.
2. Marinate the fish for 2-hours in the fridge.
3. Transfer the fish to air fryer and cook for 12-minutes at 370°F.
4. Serve with lemon slices.

Crispy Salmon Sticks

Prep time: 15 minutes | Cook time:10 minutes |Serves 4

- 1 egg, beaten
- 1/2 cup all-purpose flour

- Sea salt and ground black pepper, to taste
- 1 teaspoon hot paprika
- 1/2 cup seasoned breadcrumbs
- 1 tablespoon olive oil
- 1 pound salmon strips

1. In a mixing bowl, thoroughly combine the egg, flour, and spices. In a separate bowl, thoroughly combine the breadcrumbs and olive oil.
2. Mix to combine well.
3. Now, dip the salmon strips into the flour mixture to coat and roll the fish pieces over the breadcrumb mixture until they are well coated on all sides.
4. Cook the salmon strips at 400 °F for 10 minutes, turning them over halfway through the cooking time.
5. Bon appétit!

Basil Scallops

Prep time:15 minutes |Cook time: 6 minutes |Serves 4

- 12 oz scallops
- 1 tablespoon dried basil
- ½ teaspcon salt
- 1 tablespoon coconut oil, melted

1. Mix up salt, coconut oil, and dried basil.
2. Brush the scallops with basil mixture and leave for 5 minutes to marinate.
3. Meanwhile, preheat the air fryer to 400°F.
4. Put the marinated scallops in the air fryer and sprinkle them with remaining coconut oil and basil mixture.
5. Cook the scallops for 4 minutes.
6. Then flip them on another side and cook for 2 minutes more.

Creamed Shrimp Salad

Prep time: 10 minutes | Cook time:6 minutes |Serves 4

- 1 ½ pounds shrimp, peeled and deveined
- 1 tablespoon olive oil
- Sea salt and freshly ground black pepper, to taste
- 1 teaspoon fresh dill, chopped
- 1 teaspoon fresh basil, chopped
- 1 tablespoon fresh parsley, chopped
- 2 tablespoons chives, chopped
- 1 bell pepper, seeded and chopped
- 1 celery stalk, trimmed and chopped
- 1/2 cup mayonnaise
- 1 teaspoon stone-ground mustard
- 1 tablespoon fresh lime juice

1. Toss the shrimp and olive oil in the Air Fryer cooking basket.
2. Cook the shrimp at 400 °F for 6 minutes, tossing the basket halfway through the cooking time.
3. Place the shrimp in a salad bowl | add in the remaining ingredients and gently stir to combine. Serve well-chilled.
4. Bon appétit!

Halibut Steaks

Prep time: 15 minutes |Cook time: 10 minutes |Serves 4

- 24 oz halibut steaks (6 oz each fillet)
- ½ teaspoon salt
- ½ teaspoon ground black pepper
- 4 oz bacon, sliced
- 1 tablespoon sunflower oil

4. Cut every halibut fillet on 2 parts and sprinkle with salt and ground black pepper. Then wrap the fish fillets in the sliced bacon.
5. Preheat the air fryer to 400°F. Sprinkle the halibut bites with sunflower oil and put in the air fryer basket.
6. Cook the meal for 5 minutes. Then flip the fish bites on another side and cook them for 5 minutes more.

Sweet Tilapia Fillets

Prep time: 5 minutes | Cook time: 14 minutes |Serves 4

- 2 tablespoons Erythritol
- 1 tablespoon apple cider vinegar
- 4 tilapia fillets, boneless
- 1 teaspoon olive oil

1. Mix apple cider vinegar with olive oil and Erythritol.
2. Then rub the tilapia fillets with the sweet mixture and put in the air fryer basket in one layer.
3. Cook the fish at 380°F for 7 minutes per side.

Lemon Halibut

Prep time: 10 minutes | Cook time: 20 minutes | Serves 4

- 4 halibut fillets
- 1 egg, beaten
- 1 lemon, sliced
- salt and pepper to taste
- 1 tablespoon parsley, chopped

1. Sprinkle the lemon juice over the halibut fillets. In a food processor mix the lemon slices, salt, pepper, and parsley.
2. Take fillets and coat them with this mixture; then dip fillets into beaten egg. Cook fillets in your air fryer at 350°F for 15-minutes.

Cilantro Garlic Swordfish

Prep time: 15 minutes | Cook time:10 minutes |Serves 4

- 1 pound swordfish steaks
- 4 garlic cloves, peeled
- 4 tablespoons olive oil
- 2 tablespoons fresh lemon juice, more for later
- 1 tablespoon fresh cilantro, roughly chopped
- 1 teaspoon Spanish paprika
- Sea salt and ground black pepper, to taste

1. Toss the swordfish steaks with the remaining ingredients and place them in a lightly oiled Air Fryer cooking basket.
2. Cook the swordfish steaks at 400 °F for about 10 minutes, turning them over halfway through the cooking time.
3. Bon appétit!

Shrimp Vinaigrette

Prep time: 5 minutes | Cook time: 12 minutes |Serves 4

- 1-pound shrimps, peeled
- 3 tablespoons apple cider vinegar
- 1 teaspoon ground black pepper
- 1 teaspoon dried dill
- 1 jalapeno, chopped
- 1 tablespoon avocado oil

1. Mix shrimps with all remaining ingredients and put in the air fryer.
2. Cook the shrimps at 350°F for 12 minutes.

Chili and Oregano Tilapia

Prep time: 5 minutes | Cook time: 20 minutes |Serves 4

- 4 tilapia fillets, boneless
- 1 teaspoon chili flakes
- 1 teaspoon dried oregano
- 1 tablespoon avocado oil
- 1 teaspoon mustard

1. Rub the tilapia fillets with chili flakes, dried oregano, avocado oil, and mustard and put in the air fryer.
2. Cook it for 10 minutes per side at 380°F.

Air Fried Catfish

Prep time: 5 minutes | Cook time: 20 minutes | Serves 2

- 5 catfish filets
- 1 pinch of salt
- 1 teaspoon garlic powder
- 1 teaspoon crab seasoning
- 1 cup almond flour
- 2 tablespoons olive oil for spraying
- 2 tablespoons hot sauce
- 1 cup buttermilk
- Black pepper as needed

1. Season catfish fillets on both sides with salt and pepper.
2. In a dish, combine the buttermilk with hot sauce.
3. Add the catfish fillets and cover them with liquid.
4. Let the ingredients soak while you prepare the rest of the ingredients.
5. Whisk the flour, crab seasoning, and garlic powder in a casserole dish.
6. Remove the catfish from the buttermilk and allow excess liquid to drip off.
7. Dredge the catfish on both sides in the flour mixture.
8. Place fillets into air fryer and drizzle with oil.
9. Cook at 390°F for 15-minutes.
10. When cooking is completed remove basket and gently turn the fillets over, spray some oil on them, and cook for an additional 5-minutes.

Tuna Stuffed Avocado

Prep time: 15 minutes |Cook time: 12 minutes |Serves 2

- 1 avocado, pitted, halved
- ½ pound smoked tuna, boneless and shredded
- 1 egg, beaten
- ½ teaspoon salt
- ½ teaspoon chili powder
- ½ teaspoon ground nutmeg
- 1 teaspoon dried parsley
- cooking spray

1. Scoop ½ part of the avocado meat from the avocado to get the avocado boats. Use the scooper for this step. After this, in the mixing bowl mix up tuna and egg.
2. Shred the mixture with the help of the fork. Add salt, chili powder, ground nutmeg, and dried parsley.
3. Stir the tuna mixture until homogenous. Add the scooped avocado meat and mix up the mixture well. Fill the avocado boats with tuna mixture.
4. Preheat the air fryer to 325°F. Arrange the tuna boats in the air fryer basket and cook them for 12 minutes.

Creamy Haddock

Prep time: 10 minutes | Cook time: 8 minutes |Serves 4

- 1-pound haddock fillet
- 1 teaspoon cayenne pepper
- 1 teaspoon salt
- 1 teaspoon coconut oil
- ½ cup heavy cream

1. Grease the baking pan with coconut oil.
2. Then put haddock fillet inside and sprinkle it with cayenne pepper, salt, and heavy cream.
3. Put the baking pan in the air fryer basket and cook at 375°F for 8 minutes.

Perfect Haddock Fishcakes

Prep time: 15 minutes | Cook time:14 minutes |Serves 4

- 1 pound haddock, boneless and
- 1/4 cup all-purpose flour
- 2 eggs
- 1/2 cup parmesan cheese, grated
- 1/2 cup breadcrumbs
- 4 brioche buns

1. Mix all ingredients, except for the brioche buns, in a bowl. Shape the mixture into four patties and place them in a lightly oiled Air Fryer cooking basket.
2. Cook the fish patties at 400 °F for about 14 minutes, turning them over halfway through the cooking time.
3. Serve on hamburger buns and enjoy!

Chapter 5

Side Dishes and Snacks

Roasted Cauliflower with Onion

Prep time: 45 minutes | Cook time:13 minutes |Serves 4

- 3/4 pound cauliflower florets
- 1 large onion, cut into wedges
- 2 cloves garlic, pressed
- 1 tablespoon olive oil
- Sea salt and ground black pepper, to taste
- 1 teaspoon paprika

1. Toss the cauliflower florets and onion with the garlic, olive oil, and spices. Toss until they are well coated on all sides.
2. Arrange the vegetables in the Air Fryer basket.
3. Cook the vegetables at 400 °F for about 13 minutes, shaking the basket halfway through the cooking time.
4. Bon appétit!

Lettuce Wraps

Prep time: 10 minutes | Cook time: 4 minutes | Serves 12

- 12 bacon strips
- 12 lettuce leaves
- 1 tablespoon mustard
- 1 tablespoon apple cider vinegar

1. Put the bacon in the air fryer in one layer and cook at 400°F for 2 minutes per side.
2. Then sprinkle the bacon with mustard and apple cider vinegar and put on the lettuce.
3. Wrap the lettuce into rolls.

Buttery Garlicky Potatoes

Prep time: 20 minutes | Cook time:18 minutes |Serves 3

- 3/4 pound potatoes, quartered
- 1 tablespoon butter, melted
- 1 teaspoon garlic, pressed
- 1 teaspoon dried oregano
- Sea salt and ground black pepper, to taste

1. Toss the potatoes with the remaining ingredients until well coated on all sides.
2. Arrange the potatoes in the Air Fryer basket.
3. Cook the potatoes at 400 °F for about 18 minutes, shaking the basket halfway through the cooking time.
4. Serve warm and enjoy!

Broccoli Tots

Prep time: 15 minutes | Cook time: 8 minutes |Serves 4

- 1 teaspoon mascarpone
- 5 oz Cheddar cheese, shredded
- 3 cups broccoli, chopped, boiled
- ¼ teaspoon onion powder
- 1 teaspoon avocado oil

1. In the mixing bowl mix mascarpone with Cheddar cheese, broccoli, and onion powder.
2. Make the broccoli tots from the mixture and put them in the air fryer basket in one layer.
3. Sprinkle the broccoli tots with avocado oil and cook them at 400°F for 8 minutes.

Butter Green Beans

Prep time: 5 minutes |Cook time: 20 minutes |Serves 4

- 10 ounces green beans, trimmed
- a pinch of salt and black pepper
- 3 ounces butter, melted
- 1 cup coconut cream
- zest of ½ lemon, grated
- ¼ cup parsley, chopped
- 2 garlic cloves, minced

1. In a bowl, the butter with all the ingredients except the green beans and whisk really well.
2. Put the green beans in a pan that fits the air fryer, drizzle the buttery sauce all over, introduce the pan in the machine and cook at 370 °F for 20 minutes.
3. Divide between plates and serve as a side dish.

Charred Bell Peppers

Prep time: 5 minutes | Cook time: 4 minutes | Serves 3

- 20 bell peppers, sliced and seeded
- 1 teaspoon olive oil
- 1 pinch of sea salt
- 1 lemon

1. Preheat your air fryer to 390°F.
2. Sprinkle the peppers with oil and salt.
3. Cook the peppers in air fryer for 4-minutes.
4. Place peppers in a large bowl, and squeeze lemon juice over the top.
5. Season with salt and pepper.

Garlic Tomatoes

Prep time: 5 minutes | Cook time: 15 minutes | Serves 4

- 3 tablespoons of vinegar

- ½ teaspoon thyme, dried
- 4 tomatoes
- 1 tablespoon olive oil
- Salt and black pepper to taste
- 1 clove of garlic, minced

1. Preheat your air fryer to 390°F.
2. Cut the tomatoes into halves and remove the seeds.
3. Place them in a big bowl and toss with oil, salt, pepper, garlic, and thyme.
4. Place them into air fryer and cook for 15-minutes.
5. Drizzle with vinegar and serve.

Crunchy Bacon

Prep time: 5 minutes | Cook time: 8 minutes | Serves 4

- 8 bacon slices
- 1 teaspoon Erythritol

1. Sprinkle the bacon with Erythritol and put in the air fryer basket in one layer.
2. Cook it for 4 minutes per side or until the bacon is crunchy.

Spinach Salad

Prep time: 5 minutes |Cook time: 10 minutes |Serves 4

- 1 pound baby spinach
- salt and black pepper to the taste
- 1 tablespoon mustard
- cooking spray
- ¼ cup apple cider vinegar
- 1 tablespoon chives, chopped

1. Grease a pan that fits your air fryer with cooking spray, combine all the ingredients, introduce the pan in the fryer and cook at 350 °F for 10 minutes.
2. Divide between plates and serve as a side dish.

Sweet Potato Chips

Prep time: 10 minutes | Cook time: 15 minutes | Serves 2

- 2 large sweet potatoes, thinly sliced with mandoline
- 2 tablespoons olive oil
- salt to taste

1. Preheat your air fryer to 350°F. Stir the sweet potato slices, in a large bowl with the oil.
2. Arrange slices in your air fryer and cook them until crispy, for about 15-minutes.

Chili Zucchini Balls

Prep time: 10 minutes |Cook time: 12 minutes |Serves 4

- ¼ teaspoon salt
- ¼ teaspoon ground cumin
- 1 zucchini, grated
- 2 oz provolone cheese, grated
- ¼ teaspoon chili flakes
- 1 egg, beaten
- ¼ cup coconut flour
- 1 teaspoon sunflower oil

1. In the bowl mix up salt, ground cumin, zucchini, Provolone cheese, chili flakes, egg, and coconut flour.
2. Stir the mass with the help of the spoon and make the small balls. Then line the air fryer basket with baking paper and sprinkle it with sunflower oil.
3. Put the zucchini balls in the air fryer basket and cook them for 12 minutes at 375°F.
4. Shake the balls every 2 minutes to avoid burning.

Chili Zucchini Tots

Prep time: 10 minutes | Cook time: 12 minutes |Serves 4

- 3 zucchinis, grated
- ½ cup coconut flour
- 2 eggs, beaten
- 1 teaspoon chili flakes
- 1 teaspoon salt
- 1 teaspoon avocado oil

1. In the bowl mix up grated carrot, salt, ground cumin, zucchini, Provolone cheese, chili flakes, egg, and coconut flour. Stir the mass with the help of the spoon and make the small balls.
2. Then line the air fryer basket with baking paper and sprinkle it with sunflower oil. Put the zucchini balls in the air fryer basket and cook them for 12 minutes at 375°F. Shake the balls every 2 minutes to avoid burning.

Coconut Chips

Prep time: 10 minutes | Cook time: 5 minutes | Serves 2

- 2 cups large pieces of shredded coconut
- 1/3 teaspoon liquid stevia
- 1 tablespoon chili powder

1. Preheat your air fryer to 390°F. Combine the shredded coconut pieces with spices.
2. Cook for 5-minutes in air fryer and enjoy!

Turmeric Cauliflower

Prep time: 10 minutes |Cook time: 8 minutes |Serves 4

- 1-pound cauliflower head
- 1 tablespoon ground turmeric
- 1 tablespoon coconut oil
- ½ teaspoon dried cilantro
- ¼ teaspoon salt

1. Slice the cauliflower head on 4 steaks. Then rub every cauliflower steak with dried cilantro, salt, and ground turmeric. Sprinkle the steaks with coconut oil.
2. Preheat the air fryer to 400°F.
3. Place the cauliflower steaks in the air fryer basket and cook for 4 minutes from each side.

Herbed Cauliflower Florets

Prep time: 15 minutes | Cook time:13 minutes |Serves 3

- 3/4 pound cauliflower florets
- 1 tablespoon olive oil
- 1/2 teaspoon dried oregano
- 1 teaspoon dried basil
- 1 teaspoon dried rosemary
- Sea salt and ground black pepper, to taste

1. Toss the cauliflower florets and onion with the olive oil and spices. Toss until they are well coated on all sides.
2. Arrange the cauliflower florets in the Air Fryer basket.
3. Cook the cauliflower florets at 400 °F for about 13 minutes, shaking the basket halfway through the cooking time.
4. Bon appétit!

Mushroom Stew

Prep time: 15 minutes | Cook time: 1 hour and 22 minutes | Serves 6

- 1 lb. of chicken, cubed, boneless, skinless
- 2 tablespoons of canola oil
- 1 lb. fresh mushrooms, sliced
- 1 tablespoon thyme, dried
- ¾ cup of water
- 2 tablespoons tomato paste
- 3 large tomatoes, chopped
- 4 cloves garlic, minced
- 1 cup green peppers, sliced
- 3 cups of zucchini, diced
- 1 large onion, diced
- 1 tablespoon basil
- 1 tablespoon marjoram
- 1 tablespoon oregano

1. Cut the chicken into cubes.
2. Arrange them in the air fryer basket and pour olive oil over them.
3. Add mushrooms, zucchini, onion, and green pepper.
4. Mix and add in garlic, cook for 2-minutes, then add in tomato paste, water, and seasonings.
5. Lock the air fryer and cook the stew for 50-minutes.
6. Set the heat to 340°F and cook for an additional 20-minutes.
7. Remove from air fryer and transfer into a large pan.
8. Pour in a bit of water and simmer for 10-minutes.

Vegetable Spring Rolls

Prep time: 10 minutes | Cook time: 23 minutes | Serves 10

- 10 spring roll wrappers
- 2 tablespoons cornstarch
- water
- 3 green onions, thinly sliced
- 1 tablespoon black pepper
- 1 teaspoon soy sauce
- pinches of salt
- 2 tablespoons cooking oil, plus more for brushing
- 8-cloves of garlic, minced
- ½ bell pepper, cut into thin matchsticks
- 2 large onions, cut into thin matchsticks
- 1 large carrot, cut into thin matchsticks
- 2 cups cabbage, shredded
- 2-inch piece of ginger, grated

1. To prepare the filling: add to a large bowl the carrot, bell pepper, onion, cabbage, ginger, and garlic. Gently add two tablespoons of olive oil in a pan over high heat. Add the filling mixture and stir in salt and a dash of stevia sweetener if you like. Cook for 3-minutes. Add soy sauce, black pepper and mix well.
2. Add green onions, stir and set aside. In a small bowl, combine enough water and cornstarch to make a creamy paste. Fill the rolls with a tablespoon of filling in center of each wrapper and roll tightly, dampening the edges with cornstarch paste to ensure a good seal. Repeat until all wrappers and filling are used.
3. Preheat your air fryer to 350°F. Brush the rolls with oil, and arrange them in the air fryer, and cook them until crisp and golden for about 20-minutes. Halfway through the cook time flip them over.

Chives and Spinach

Prep time: 5 minutes | Cook time: 10 minutes |Serves 4

- 3 cups spinach, chopped
- 1 oz chives, chopped
- ½ cup heavy cream
- 1 teaspoon chili powder

1. Mix spinach with chives, heavy cream, and chili powder.
2. Put the mixture in the air fryer basket and cook at 380°F for 10 minutes.
3. Carefully mix the meal before serving.

Tomato and Cheese Stuffed Peppers

Prep time: 13 minutes | Cook time:10 minutes |Serves 3

- 3 bell peppers, seeded and halved
- 1 tablespoon olive oil
- 1 small onion, chopped
- 2 garlic cloves, minced
- Sea salt and ground black pepper, to taste
- 1 cup tomato sauce
- 2 ounces cheddar cheese, shredded

1. Toss the peppers with the oil and place them in the Air Fryer cooking basket.
2. Mix the onion, garlic, salt, black pepper, and tomato sauce. Spoon the sauce into the pepper halves.
3. Cook the peppers at 400 °F for about 10 minutes. Top the peppers with the cheese. Continue to cook for 5 minutes more.
4. Bon appétit!

Carrot Chips

**Prep time: 10 minutes | Cook time: 13 minutes |
Serves 8**

- 3 carrots, thinly sliced
- 1 teaspoon avocado oil

1. Put the carrots in the air fryer basket, sprinkle with avocado oil.
2. Cook the carrot chips for 30 minutes at 355°F. Shake the carrot chips every 5 minutes.

Carrots with Sesame Seeds

Prep time: 20 minutes | Cook time:15 minutes |Serves 3

- 3/4 pound carrots, trimmed and cut into sticks
- 2 tablespoons butter, melted
- Coarse sea salt and white pepper, to taste
- 1 tablespoon sesame seeds, lightly toasted

1. Toss the carrots with the butter, salt, and white pepper | then, arrange them in the Air Fryer basket.
2. Cook the carrots at 380 °F for 15 minutes and make sure to check the carrots halfway through the cooking time.
3. Top the carrots with the sesame seeds. Bon appétit!

Zucchini Nests

Prep time: 15 minutes |Cook time: 6 minutes |Serves 6

- 10 oz zucchini, grated
- 4 quail eggs
- 1 tablespoon coconut flour
- 1 oz parmesan, grated
- ¼ teaspoon cayenne pepper
- 1 teaspoon butter, melted
-

1. Brush the muffin molds with butter. Then mix up cayenne pepper and grated zucchini.
2. Put the vegetable mixture in the muffin molds and flatten it in the shape of the nests.
3. After this, crack the quail eggs in the nests and sprinkle with grated Parmesan. Preheat the air fryer to 390°F.
4. Put the muffin molds with nests in the air fryer basket and cook for 6 minutes.

Butter Garlic Brussels Sprouts

Prep time: 15 minutes | Cook time:14 minutes |Serves 3

- 3/4 pound Brussels sprouts
- 2 tablespoons butter, melted
- 2 garlic cloves, crushed
- Kosher salt and ground black pepper, to taste

1. Toss the Brussels sprouts with the remaining ingredients until well coated.
2. Arrange the Brussels sprouts in the Air Fryer basket.
3. Cook the Brussels sprouts at 380 °F for 14 minutes, shaking the basket halfway through the cooking time.
4. Bon appétit!

Easy Roasted Eggplant

Prep time: 18 minutes | Cook time:15 minutes |Serves 3

- 3/4 pound eggplant, peeled and diced
- 2 tablespoons sesame oil
- 1/2 teaspoon cumin powder
- 1/2 teaspoon onion powder
- 1 teaspoon granulated garlic

1. Toss the eggplant pieces with the remaining ingredients until they are well coated on all sides.
2. Arrange the eggplant in the Air Fryer basket.
3. Cook the potatoes at 400 °F for about 15 minutes, shaking the basket halfway through the cooking time.
4. Garnish with fresh herbs, if desired. Bon appétit!

Yellow Beans with Tomatoes

Prep time: 9 minutes | Cook time:8 minutes |Serves 3

- 1/2 pound yellow beans, trimmed
- 2 small tomatoes, sliced
- 1 tablespoon sesame oil
- Sea salt and ground black pepper, to taste

1. Toss the green beans and tomatoes with the olive oil, salt, and black pepper and toss until they are well coated.
2. Arrange the vegetables in the Air Fryer basket.
3. Cook the green beans at 390 °F for 8 minutes and make sure to stir your vegetables halfway through the cooking time.
4. Taste, adjust the seasonings, and serve immediately. Bon appétit!

Chapter 6

Vegan & Vegetarian

Basic Fried Cucumber

Prep time: 20 minutes | Cook time:15 minutes
|Serves 4

- 2 cucumbers, sliced
- 2 tablespoons olive oil
- 1/2 cup cornmeal
- Sea salt and ground black pepper, to taste

1. Toss the cucumbers with the remaining ingredients and place them in the Air Fryer cooking basket.
2. Cook the cucumbers at 400 °F for about 15 minutes, shaking the basket occasionally to ensure even cooking.
3. Serve warm and enjoy!

Rosemary Orange Beets

Prep time: 35 minutes | Cook time:30 minutes
|Serves 3

- 1 pound beets, peeled and diced
- 2 tablespoons olive oil
- Sea salt and ground black pepper, to taste
- 1 tablespoon stone-ground mustard
- 2 tablespoons balsamic vinegar
- 1/4 cup fresh orange juice
- 1 tablespoon fresh rosemary, chopped

1. Toss the red beets with the remaining ingredients until well coated on all sides.
2. Air fry the red beets at 390 °F for about 30 minutes, tossing the basket every 10 minutes to ensure even cooking.
3. Bon appétit!

Carrot & Zucchini Muffins

Prep time: 8 minutes | Cook time: 14 minutes |
Serves 4

- 2 tablespoons butter, melted
- ¼ cup carrots, shredded
- ½ cup zucchini, shredded
- 1 ½ cups almond flour

- 1 tablespoon liquid Stevia
- 2 teaspoons baking powder
- Pinch of salt
- 3 eggs
- 1 tablespoon yogurt
- 1 cup milk

1. Preheat your air fryer to 350°F.
2. Beat the eggs, yogurt, milk, salt, pepper, baking soda, and Stevia.
3. Whisk in the flour gradually.
4. Add zucchini and carrots.
5. Grease muffin tins with butter and pour muffin batter into tins.
6. Cook for 14-minutes and serve.

Chili Fried Brussels Sprouts

Prep time: 10 minutes |Cook time: 15 minutes |Serves 5

- 1-pound brussels sprouts
- 1 teaspoon chili flakes
- 3 eggs, beaten
- 3 tablespoons coconut flakes
- 1 teaspoon salt
- 1 teaspoon sesame oil

1. Cut Brussels sprouts into halves and put them in the bowl. Add chili flakes, eggs, and salt.
2. Shake the vegetables well and then sprinkle them with coconut flakes. Shake the vegetables well. Preheat the air fryer to 325°F.
3. Put Brussels sprouts in the air fryer and cook them for 10 minutes.
4. Then shake the vegetables well and cook for 5 minutes more.

Vegetarian Hash Browns

Prep time: 8 minutes | Cook time: 19 minutes | Serves 8

- 4 large potatoes, peeled, shredded
- 1 teaspoon onion powder
- 1 teaspoon garlic powder
- 2 teaspoons chili flakes
- Salt and pepper to taste
- 2 tablespoons corn flour
- 2 teaspoons olive oil
- Cooking spray as needed

1. Add potatoes to a bowl of cold water and leave them to soak for a few minutes then drain them and repeat.
2. Add a teaspoon of olive oil into skillet and cook potatoes over medium heat for 4-minutes.
3. Place potatoes on plate to cool once they are cooked.
4. In a large mixing bowl, add flour, potatoes, salt, pepper and other seasonings and combine well.
5. Place bowl in fridge for 20-minutes.
6. Preheat your air fryer to 350°F.
7. Remove hash browns from fridge and cut into size pieces you desire.
8. Spray the wire basket of your air fryer with some oil, add the hash browns and fry them for 15-minutes.
9. Halfway through flip them to help cook them all over. Serve hot!

Herbed Asparagus and Sauce

Prep time:4 minutes |Cook time: 10 minutes |Serves 4

- 1 pound asparagus, trimmed
- 2 tablespoons olive oil Apinch of salt and black pepper
- 1 teaspoon garlic powder
- 1 teaspoon oregano, dried
- 1 cup Greek yogurt
- 1 cup basil, chopped
- ½ cup parsley, chopped
- ¼ cup chives, chopped
- ¼ cup lemon juice
- 2 garlic cloves, minced

1. In a bowl, mix the asparagus with the oil, salt, pepper, oregano and garlic powder, and toss.
2. Put the asparagus in the air fryer's basket and cook at 400 °F for 10 minutes.
3. Meanwhile, in a blender, mix the yogurt with basil, chives, parsley, lemon juice and garlic cloves and pulse well.
4. Divide the asparagus between plates, drizzle the sauce all over and serve.

Roasted Sweet Potatoes

Prep time: 40 minutes | Cook time:35 minutes |Serves 3

- 1 pound sweet potatoes, cubed
- 2 tablespoons coconut oil
- Kosher salt and freshly ground black pepper, to taste
- 1 teaspoon garlic, minced
- 1/2 teaspoon ground cumin
- 2 tablespoons fresh coriander, chopped
- 2 tablespoons fresh parsley, chopped
- 2 tablespoons fresh scallions, chopped

1. Toss the sweet potatoes with the remaining ingredients.
2. Cook the sweet potatoes at 380 °F for 35 minutes, shaking the basket halfway through the cooking time.
3. Taste and adjust the seasonings. Bon appétit!

Cheesy Green Patties

Prep time:20 minutes |Cook time: 6 minutes |Serves 2

- 1 ½ cup fresh spinach, chopped
- 3 oz provolone cheese, shredded
- 1 egg, beaten
- ¼ cup almond flour
- ½ teaspoon salt
- Cooking spray

1. Put the chopped spinach in the blender and blend it until you get a smooth mixture.
2. After this, transfer the grinded spinach in the big bowl.
3. Add shredded provolone cheese, beaten egg, almond flour, and salt.
4. Stir the spinach mixture with the help of the spoon until it is homogenous.
5. Then make the patties from the spinach mixture.

6. Preheat the air fryer to 400°F.
7. Spray the air fryer basket with cooking spray from inside and put the spinach patties.
8. Cook them for 3 minutes and then flip on another side.
9. Cook the patties for 3 minutes more or until they are light brown.

Balsamic Asparagus and Tomatoes

Prep time: 5 minutes |Cook time: 10 minutes |Serves 4

- 1 pound asparagus, trimmed
- 2 cups cherry tomatoes, halved
- ¼ cup parmesan, grated
- ½ cup balsamic vinegar
- 2 tablespoons olive oil
- a pinch of salt and black pepper

1. In a bowl, mix the asparagus with the rest of the ingredients except the parmesan, and toss.
2. Put the asparagus and tomatoes in your air fryer's basket and cook at 400 °F for 10 minutes Divide between plates and serve with the parmesan sprinkled on top.

Green Beans and Tomato Sauce

Prep time: 5 minutes |Cook time: 15 minutes |Serves 4

- ½ pound green beans, trimmed and halved
- 1 cup black olives, pitted and halved
- ¼ cup bacon, cooked and crumbled
- 1 tablespoon olive oil
- ¼ cup keto tomato sauce

1. In a pan that fits the air fryer, combine all the ingredients, toss, put the pan in the air fryer and cook at 380 °F for 15 minutes.
2. Divide between plates and serve.

Spicy Roasted Cabbage

Prep time: 10 minutes | Cook time:7 minutes |Serves 4

- 1 pound cabbage, cut into wedges
- 1 teaspoon garlic, minced
- 2 tablespoons olive oil
- 1 teaspoon red pepper flakes
- Sea salt and ground black pepper, to taste

1. Toss the cabbage wedges with the remaining ingredients.
2. Cook the cabbage wedges at 350 °F for 7 minutes, shaking the basket halfway through the cooking time.
3. Taste and adjust the seasonings. Bon appétit!

Turmeric Zucchini Patties

Prep time:15 minutes |Cook time: 10 minutes |Serves 4

- 2 zucchinis, trimmed, grated
- 1 egg yolk
- ½ teaspoon salt
- 1 teaspoon ground turmeric
- ½ teaspoon ground paprika
- 1 teaspoon cream cheese
- 3 tablespoons flax meal
- 1 teaspoon sesame oil

1. Squeeze the juice from the zucchinis and put them in the big bowl.
2. Add egg yolk, salt, ground turmeric, ground paprika, flax meal, and cream cheese.
3. Stir the mixture well with the help of the spoon.
4. Then make medium size patties from the zucchini mixture.
5. Preheat the air fryer to 325°F.
6. Brush the air fryer basket with sesame oil and put the patties inside.
7. Cook them for 5 minutes from each side.

Parsley and Garlic Roasted Peppers

Prep time: 20 minutes | Cook time:15 minutes |Serves 2

- 4 bell peppers, seeded and halved lengthwise
- 2 tablespoons olive oil
- 1 tablespoon fresh parsley, chopped
- 2 cloves garlic, minced
- Sea salt and ground black pepper, to taste

1. Toss the peppers with the remaining ingredients | place them in the Air Fryer cooking basket.
2. Cook the peppers at 400 °F for about 15 minutes, shaking the basket halfway through the cooking time.
3. Taste, adjust the seasonings and serve at room temperature. Bon appétit!

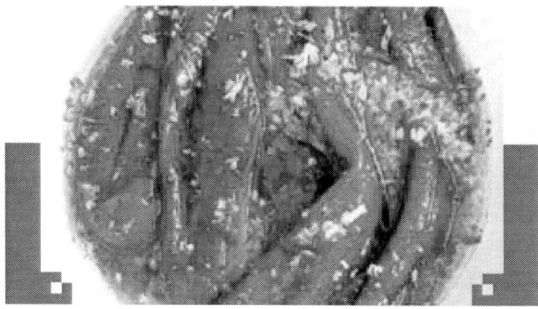

Mozzarella Green Beans

Prep time: 10 minutes |Cook time: 6 minutes |Serves 4

- 1 cup green beans, trimmed
- 2 oz mozzarella, shredded
- 1 teaspoon butter
- ½ teaspoon chili flakes
- ¼ cup beef broth

1. Sprinkle the green beans with chili flakes and put in the air fryer baking pan.
2. Add beef broth and butter.
3. Then top the vegetables with shredded Mozzarella. Preheat the air fryer to 400°F.
4. Put the pan with green beans in the air fryer and cook the meal for 6 minutes.

Mom's Famous Chickpea Burgers

Prep time: 20 minutes | Cook time:15 minutes |Serves 4

- 16 ounces canned chickpeas, drained and rinsed
- 1/4 cup flaxseeds, ground
- 2 garlic cloves, minced
- 1 medium-sized onion, chopped
- 2 tablespoons fresh lemon juice
- 2 tablespoons olive oil
- 1/2 teaspoon ground cumin
- 1/4 teaspoon ground allspice
- Sea salt and ground black pepper, to taste

1. Pulse all ingredients in your food processor until everything is well incorporated.
2. Toss the beets with the remaining ingredients and place them in the Air Fryer cooking basket.
3. Cook the burgers at 380 °F for about 15 minutes, turning them over halfway

through the cooking time.

4. Bon appétit!

Vegan Cheese Stuffed Peppers

Prep time:20 minutes | Cook time:15 minutes |Serves 3

- 6 Italian peppers, seeded and stems removed
- 2 garlic cloves, minced
- 1 tablespoon taco seasoning mix
- 1/2 cup vegan cheddar cheese, grated
- Sea salt and red pepper flakes, to taste
- 2 tablespoons olive oil

1. Arrange the peppers in the Air Fryer cooking basket.
2. Mix the remaining ingredients until well combined. Dived the filling between the peppers.
3. Cook the peppers at 400 °F for about 15 minutes.
4. Bon appétit!

Greek-Style Stuffed Zucchini

Prep time: 15 minutes | Cook time:10 minutes |Serves 2

- 2 medium zucchinis, halved
- 2 tablespoons olive oil
- 1 shallot, chopped
- 2 garlic cloves, minced
- 1 small tomato, chopped
- 1 teaspoon hot sauce
- 1 teaspoon tamari sauce
- Sea salt and ground black pepper, to taste

1. Place the zucchini halves in a lightly oiled Air Fryer cooking basket.
2. Mix the remaining ingredients to make the filling | stuff the zucchini halves with the prepared filling.
3. Cook the zucchini at 390 °F for 10 minutes or until cooked through.
4. Bon appétit!

Herbed Baby Potatoes

Prep time: 25 minutes | Cook time:20 minutes |Serves 3

- 1 pound baby potatoes
- 2 tablespoons olive oil
- 1 teaspoon dried thyme
- 1 teaspoon dried rosemary
- 1 teaspoon dried basil
- 1 teaspoon dried oregano
- 1 teaspoon dried parsley flakes
- 1 teaspoon garlic, minced
- Sea salt and ground black pepper, to taste
- 1 teaspoon cayenne pepper

1. Toss the potatoes with the remaining ingredients until well coated on all sides.
2. Arrange the potatoes in the Air Fryer basket.
3. Cook the potatoes at 400 °F for about 20 minutes, shaking the basket halfway through the cooking time.
4. Bon appétit!

Chapter 7

Appetizers

Golden Beet Chips

Prep time: 35 minutes | Cook time:30 minutes |Serves 2

- 1/2 pound golden beets, peeled and thinly sliced
- Kosher salt and ground black pepper, to taste
- 1 teaspoon paprika
- 2 tablespoons olive oil
- 1/2 teaspoon garlic powder
- 1 teaspoon ground turmeric

1. Start by preheating your Air Fryer to 330 °F.
2. Toss the beets with the remaining ingredients and place them in the Air Fryer cooking basket.
3. Air fry your chips for 30 minutes, shaking the basket occasionally and working in batches.
4. Enjoy!

Parmesan Asparagus Fries

Prep time: 10 minutes | Cook time: 10 minutes | Serves 5

- 1 lb. asparagus spears
- ¼ cup almond flour
- salt and pepper to taste
- 2 eggs, beaten
- ½ cup parmesan cheese, grated
- 1 cup pork rinds

1. Preheat your air fryer to 380°F. Combine pork rinds and parmesan cheese in a small bowl. Season with salt and pepper. Line baking sheet with parchment paper. First, dip half the asparagus spears into flour, then into eggs, and finally into pork rind mixture.
2. Place asparagus spears on the baking sheet and bake for 10-minutes. Repeat with remaining spears.

Chopped Liver with Eggs

Prep time: 10 minutes | Cook time: 12 minutes | Serves 2

- 2 large eggs
- 1 lb. sliced liver
- salt and pepper to taste
- 1 tablespoon cream
- ½ tablespoon black truffle oil
- 1 tablespoon butter

1. Preheat your air fryer to 340°F. Cut liver into thin slices and place in the fridge. Separate the whites from the yolks of the eggs and put each yolk in a cup. In another bowl, add the cream, the black truffle oil, salt, pepper and beat to combine.
2. Take the liver and arrange half of the mixture in a small ramekin. Pour the white of the egg and divide equally between two ramekins. Put the yolks on top. Surround the yolks with the liver and cook for 12-minutes. Serve cool.

Chilies Casserole

Prep time: 10 minutes | Cook time: 15 minutes | Serves 2

- 1 chili pepper, chopped
- 1 cup ground chicken
- ¼ cup Mozzarella, shredded
- ½ teaspoon ground cinnamon
- ½ teaspoon coconut oil
- ¼ cup cauliflower, chopped

1. Mix chili pepper with ground chicken, Mozzarella, ground cinnamon, and cauliflower.
2. Brush the air fryer basket with coconut oil and put the mixture inside.
3. Bake the casserole at 375°F for 15 minutes.

Almond Milk Bake

Prep time: 5 minutes | Cook time: 25 minutes | Serves 4

- 2 cups cauliflower, roughly chopped
- 2 ounces Monterey Jack cheese, shredded
- 4 eggs, beaten
- 1 cup organic almond milk
- 1 teaspoon dried oregano

1. In the mixing bowl, mix dried oregano with almond milk and eggs.
2. Pour the liquid in the air fryer basket and add cauliflower and cheese.
3. Close the lid and cook the meal at 350°F for 25 minutes.

Baked Tomato & Egg

Prep time: 10 minutes | Cook time: 20 minutes | Serves 2

- 2 tomatoes
- 4 eggs
- 1 cup mozzarella cheese, shredded
- salt and pepper to taste
- 1 tablespoon olive oil
- a few basil leaves

1. Preheat your air fryer to 360°F. Cut each tomato into two halves and place them in a bowl. Season with salt and pepper.
2. Place cheese around the bottom of the tomatoes and add the basil leaves. Break one egg into each tomato slice. Garnish with cheese and drizzle with olive oil. Set the temperature to 360°F and bake for 20-minutes.

Walnut Bars

Prep time:5 minutes |Cook time: 16 minutes |Serves 4

- 1 egg
- 1/3 cup cocoa powder
- 3 tablespoons swerve
- 7 tablespoons ghee, melted
- 1 teaspoon vanilla extract
- ¼ cup almond flour
- ¼ cup walnuts, chopped
- ½ teaspoon baking soda

1. In a bowl, mix all the ingredients and stir well.
2. Spread this on a baking sheet that fits your air fryer lined with parchment paper, put it in the fryer and cook at 330 °F and bake for 16 minutes.
3. Leave the bars to cool down, cut and serve.

Cheddar Cheese Cauliflower Bites

Prep time: 15 minutes | Cook time:13 minutes |Serves 4

- 1 pound cauliflower, grated
- 1/2 cup cheddar cheese, shredded
- 1 ounce butter, room temperature
- Sea salt and ground black pepper, to taste
- 1/2 cup tortilla chips, crushed
- 2 eggs whisked

1. Thoroughly combine all the ingredients in a mixing bowl. Shape the mixture into bite-sized balls.
2. Cook the cauliflower balls at 350 °F for about 13 minutes, turning them over halfway through the cooking time.
3. Bon appétit!

Fried Green Tomatoes

Prep time: 20 minutes | Cook time:15 minutes |Serves 4

- 1/2 cup all-purpose flour
- Sea salt and ground black pepper, to taste
- 1 teaspoon garlic powder
- 1 teaspoon cayenne pepper
- 2 eggs
- 1/2 cup milk
- 2 tablespoons olive oil
- 1 cup breadcrumbs
- 1 pound green tomatoes, sliced

1. Start by preheating your Air Fryer to 390 °F.
2. In a shallow bowl, mix the flour, salt, black pepper, garlic powder, and cayenne pepper.
3. Whisk the egg and milk in another shallow bowl. Mix the olive oil and breadcrumbs in a separate bowl.
4. Dip the green tomatoes in the flour, then in the eggs, then in the breadcrumbs. Place the green tomatoes in the Air Fryer basket.
5. Cook the green tomatoes for about 15 minutes or until golden brown and cooked through.
6. Serve with toothpicks. Bon appétit!

Cheesy Tomato Chips

Prep time: 20 minutes | Cook time:15 minutes |Serves 3

- 1 tomato
- 2 tablespoons olive oil
- 1/2 teaspoon paprika
- Sea salt, to taste
- 1 teaspoon garlic powder
- 1 tablespoon fresh cilantro, chopped
- 4 tablespoons Pecorino cheese, grated

1. Toss the tomato slices with the olive oil and spices until they are well coated on all sides.
2. Arrange the tomato slices in the Air Fryer cooking basket.
3. Cook the tomato slices at 360 °F for about 10 minutes. Turn the temperature to 330 °F and top the tomato slices with the cheese | now, continue to cook for a further 5 minutes.
4. Bon appétit!

Lemon Garlic Eggplant Chips

Prep time: 20 minutes | Cook time:15minutes |Serves 4

- 1 pound eggplant, sliced
- 2 tablespoons olive oil
- 1 teaspoon garlic, minced
- Sea salt and ground black pepper, to taste
- 2 tablespoons lemon juice, freshly squeezed

1. Toss the eggplant pieces with the remaining ingredients until they are well coated on all sides.
2. Arrange the eggplant in the Air Fryer basket.
3. Cook the eggplant at 400 °F for about 15 minutes, shaking the basket halfway through the cooking time.
4. Bon appétit!

Cucumber Sushi

Prep time: 10 minutes |Cook time: 10 minutes |Serves10

- 10 bacon slices
- 2 tablespoons cream cheese
- 1 cucumber

1. Place the bacon slices in the air fryer in one layer and cook for 10 minutes at 400°F.
2. Meanwhile, cut the cucumber into small wedges. When the bacon is cooked, cool it to the room temperature and spread with cream cheese.
3. Then place the cucumber wedges over the cream cheese and roll the bacon into the sushi.

Spicy Mozzarella Stick

Prep time: 10 minutes | Cook time: 5 minutes | Serves 3

- 8-ounces mozzarella cheese, cut into strips
- 2 tablespoons olive oil
- ½ teaspoon salt
- 1 cup pork rinds
- 1 egg
- 1 teaspoon garlic powder
- 1 teaspoon paprika

1. Cut the mozzarella into 6 strips. Whisk the egg along with salt, paprika, and garlic powder. Dip the mozzarella strips into egg mixture first, then into pork rinds. Arrange them on a baking platter and place in the fridge for 30-minutes.
2. Preheat your air fryer to 360°F. Drizzle olive oil into the air fryer. Arrange the mozzarella sticks in the air fryer and cook for about 5-minutes. Make sure to turn them at least twice, to ensure they will become golden on all sides.

Kale Eggs

Prep time: 10 minutes | Cook time: 20 minutes | Serves 4

- 1 cup kale, chopped
- 6 eggs, beaten
- ¼ cup heavy cream
- ½ teaspoon ground black pepper
- ½ teaspoon coconut oil

1. Grease ramekins with coconut oil.
2. Then mix kale with eggs and heavy cream.
3. Add ground black pepper.
4. Pour the mixture in the ramekins and cook them in the air fryer basket at 375°F for 20 minutes.

Classic Kale Chips

Prep time: 10 minutes | Cook time:8 minutes |Serves 4

- 4 cups kale, torn into pieces
- 1 tablespoon sesame oil
- 1 teaspoon garlic powder
- Sea salt and ground black pepper, to taste

1. Start by preheating your Air Fryer to 360 °F.
2. Toss the kale leaves with the remaining ingredients and place them in the Air Fryer cooking basket.
3. Air fry your chips for 8 minutes, shaking the basket occasionally and working in batches.
4. Enjoy!

Zucchini Crackers

Prep time: 15 minutes |Cook time: 20 minutes |Serves16

- 1 cup zucchini, grated
- 2 tablespoons flax meal
- 1 teaspoon salt
- 3 tablespoons almond flour
- ¼ teaspoon baking powder
- ¼ teaspoon chili flakes
- 1 tablespoon xanthan gum
- 1 tablespoon butter, softened
- 1 egg, beaten
- cooking spray

1. Squeeze the zucchini to get rid of vegetable juice and transfer in the big bowl.
2. Add flax meal, salt, almond flour, baking powder, chili flakes, xanthan gum, and stir well. After this, add butter and egg.
3. Knead the non-sticky dough. Place it on the baking paper and cover with the second sheet of baking paper.
4. Roll up the dough into the flat square. After this, remove the baking paper from the dough surface. Cut it on medium size crackers.
5. Line the air fryer basket with baking paper and put the crackers inside in one layer.
6. Spray them with cooking spray. Cook them at 355°F for 20 minutes.

Cheesy Zucchini Chips

Prep time: 15 minutes | Cook time:10 minutes |Serves 4

- 1 pound zucchini, sliced
- 1 cup Pecorino Romano cheese, grated
- Sea salt and cayenne pepper, to taste

1. Start by preheating your Air Fryer to 390 °F.
2. Toss the zucchini slices with the remaining ingredients and arrange them in a single layer in the Air Fryer cooking basket.
3. Cook the zucchini slices for about 10 minutes at 390 °F, shaking the basket halfway through the cooking time. Work in batches.
4. Bon appétit!

Chives Meatballs

Prep time: 5 minutes |Cook time: 20 minutes |Serves 6

- 1 pound beef meat, ground
- 1 teaspoon onion powder
- 1 teaspoon garlic powder
- a pinch of salt and black pepper
- 2 tablespoons chives, chopped
- cooking spray

1. In a bowl, mix all the ingredients except the cooking spray, stir well and shape medium meatballs out of this mix.
2. Pace them in your lined air fryer's basket, grease with cooking spray and cook at 360 °F for 20 minutes. Serve as an appetizer.

Zucchinis Bars

Prep time:10 minutes |Cook time: 15 minutes |Serves 12

- 3 tablespoons coconut oil, melted
- 6 eggs
- 3 ounces zucchini, shredded
- 2 teaspoons vanilla extract
- ½ teaspoon baking powder
- 4 ounces cream cheese
- 2 tablespoons erythritol

1. In a bowl, combine all the ingredients and whisk well.
2. pour this into a baking dish that fits your air fryer lined with parchment paper, introduce in the fryer and cook at 320 °F, bake for 15 minutes.
3. Slice and serve cold.

Mushroom Pizza Bites

Prep time: 10 minutes |Cook time: 7 minutes |Serves6

- 6 cremini mushroom caps
- 3 oz parmesan, grated
- 1 tablespoon olive oil
- ½ tomato, chopped
- ½ teaspoon dried basil
- 1 teaspoon ricotta cheese

1. Preheat the air fryer to 400°F. Sprinkle the mushroom caps with olive oil and put in the air fryer basket in one layer.
2. Cook them for 3 minutes. After this, mix up tomato and ricotta cheese. Fill the mushroom caps with tomato mixture.
3. Then top them with parmesan and sprinkle with dried basil. Cook the mushroom pizzas for 4 minutes at 400°F.

Cheese and Herb Stuffed Mushrooms

Prep time: 10 minutes | Cook time:7 minutes |Serves 4

- 2 tablespoons olive oil
- 1/2 cup breadcrumbs
- 1/2 cup Parmesan cheese, grated
- 1 teaspoon garlic, minced
- 1 tablespoon fresh parsley, chopped
- 1 tablespoon fresh chives, chopped
- Sea salt and freshly ground black pepper, to taste
- 1 pound button mushrooms, stems removed

1. In a mixing bowl, thoroughly combine the olive oil, breadcrumbs, Parmesan cheese, garlic, parsley, chives, salt, and black pepper.
2. Divide the filling between your mushrooms. Arrange the mushrooms in the Air Fryer basket.
3. Cook your mushrooms at 400 °F for about 7 minutes, shaking the basket halfway through the cooking time.
4. Bon appétit!

Paprika Chips

Prep time: 2 minutes |Cook time: 5 minutes |Serves 4

- 8 ounces cheddar cheese, shredded
- 1 teaspoon sweet paprika

1. Divide the cheese in small heaps in a pan that fits the air fryer, sprinkle the paprika on top, introduce the pan in the machine and cook at 400 °F for 5 minutes.
2. Cool the chips down and serve them.

Cream Cheese Rolls

Prep time: 15 minutes | Cook time: 10 minutes | Serves 4

- 4 eggs, beaten
- ½ teaspoon coconut oil, melted
- ½ teaspoon chili flakes
- 2 tablespoons cream cheese

1. Mix eggs with chili flakes.
2. Then brush the air fryer basket with coconut oil and preheat it to 395°F.
3. Make 4 crepes from egg mixture and cook them in the air fryer basket.
4. Then spread the cream cheese over the every egg crepe and roll.

Sesame Bars

Prep time:15 minutes |Cook time: 10 minutes |Serves 6

- 1 cup coconut flour
- 2 tablespoons coconut flakes
- 2 eggs, beaten
- 1 teaspoon baking powder
- ¼ cup Erythritol
- 1 teaspoon vanilla extract
- 1 tablespoon butter, softened
- 1 teaspoon sesame seeds
- Cooking spray

1. Put coconut flour in the bowl.
2. Add coconut flakes, eggs, baking powder, Erythritol, vanilla extract, and sesame seeds.
3. Add butter.
4. Stir the mixture with the help of the spoon until it is homogenous.
5. Then roll up the dough into the square and cut into the bars.
6. Preheat the air fryer to 325°F, Line the air fryer with baking paper and put the coconut bars inside.
7. Cook the coconut bars for 10 minutes.

Mini Bacon-Wrapped Sausages

Prep time: 20 minutes | Cook time:15 minutes |Serves 4

- 1 pound mini sausages
- 2 tablespoons tamari sauce
- 2 tablespoons maple syrup
- 1 teaspoon chili powder
- Ground black pepper, to taste
- 4 ounces bacon, thinly slices

1. Toss the mini sausages with the tamari sauce, maple syrup, chili powder, and black pepper.
2. Wrap the mini sausages with the bacon.
3. Place the sausages in a lightly oiled Air Fryer cooking basket.
4. Cook the sausages at 380 °F for 15 minutes, tossing the basket halfway through the cooking time.
5. Serve warm and enjoy!

Chapter 8

Desserts

Cinnamon Apple Wedges

Prep time: 20 minutes | Cook time: 17 minutes |Serves 2

- 2 apples, peeled, cored, and cut into wedges
- 2 teaspoons coconut oil
- 2 tablespoons brown sugar
- 1 teaspoon pure vanilla extract
- 1 teaspoon ground cinnamon
- 1/4 cup water

1. Toss the apples with the coconut oil, sugar, vanilla, and cinnamon.
2. Pour 1/4 cup of water into an Air Fryer safe dish. Place the apples in the dish.
3. Bake the apples at 340 °F for 17 minutes. Serve at room temperature. Bon appétit!

Grandma's Apple Cakes

Prep time: 20 minutes | Cook time: 20 minutes |Serves 4

- 1/2 cup all-purpose flour
- 1/2 cup oats, ground
- 1/2 teaspoon baking powder
- 1 apple, peeled and grated
- 1/4 cup dried cranberries
- 2 tablespoons butter
- 1/2 teaspoon ground cinnamon
- 1/2 cup full-Fat milk
- 1 egg, whisked

1. In a mixing bowl, thoroughly combine all the ingredients.
2. Drop a spoonful of batter onto the greased Air Fryer pan. Cook in the preheated Air Fryer at 360 °F for 10 minutes, flipping them halfway through the cooking time.
3. Repeat with the remaining batter and serve warm. Enjoy!

Cream Cheese Pie

Prep time: 15 minutes | Cook time: 30 minutes |Serves 6

- 2 eggs, beaten
- 6 tablespoons almond flour
- ½ teaspoon vanilla extract
- 6 tablespoons cream cheese
- ½ teaspoon baking powder
- 1 teaspoon apple cider vinegar
- ½ teaspoon ground cinnamon
- 3 tablespoons Erythritol
- 1 tablespoon coconut oil, melted

1. Brush the baking pan with coconut oil.
2. Then mix eggs with almond flour, vanilla extract, cream cheese, baking powder, apple cider vinegar, ground cinnamon, and Erythritol.
3. Blend the mixture until smooth and pour it in the baking pan.
4. Cook the pie in the air fryer at 350°F for 30 minutes.
5. Then cool the cooked pie well.

Coconut Chocolate Cake

Prep time: 25 minutes | Cook time: 20 minutes |Serves 6

- 1/2 cup coconut oil, room temperature
- 1 cup brown sugar
- 2 chia eggs (2 tablespoons ground chia seeds + 4 tablespoons water)
- 1/4 cup all-purpose flour
- 1/4 cup coconut flour
- 1/2 cup cocoa powder
- 1/2 cup dark chocolate chips
- A pinch of grated nutmeg
- A pinch of sea salt
- 2 tablespoons coconut milk

1. Start by preheating your Air Fryer to 340 °F. Now, spritz the sides and bottom of a baking pan with a nonstick cooking spray.
2. In a mixing bowl, beat the coconut oil and brown sugar until fluffy. Next, fold in the chia eggs and beat again until well combined.
3. After that, add in the remaining ingredients. Mix until everything is well incorporated.
4. Bake in the preheated Air Fryer for 20 minutes. Enjoy!

Lemon Pie

Prep time: 10 minutes | Cook time: 35 minutes |Serves 6

- 1 cup coconut flour
- ½ lemon, sliced
- ¼ cup heavy cream
- 2 eggs, beaten
- 2 tablespoons Erythritol
- 1 teaspoon baking powder
- Cooking spray

1. Spray the air fryer basket with cooking spray.

2. Then line the bottom of the air fryer with lemon.
3. In the mixing bowl, mix coconut flour with heavy cream, eggs, Erythritol, and baking powder.
4. Pour the batter over the lemons and cook the pie at 365 °F for 35 minutes.

Creamy Crumble

Prep time: 15 minutes |Cook time: 20 minutes |Serves 4

- 4 oz rhubarb, chopped
- ¼ cup heavy cream
- 1 teaspoon ground cinnamon
- ¼ cup erythritol
- 1 cup almond flour
- 1 egg, beaten
- 1 teaspoon avocado oil
- 4 teaspoons butter, softened

1. In the bowl mix up heavy cream, ground cinnamon, almond flour, egg, and butter, Stir the mixture until you get the crumbly texture.
2. Then mix up rhubarb and Erythritol. Brush the air fryer mold with avocado oil.
3. Separate the crumbled dough on 4 parts. Put 1 part of the dough in the air fryer mold.
4. Then sprinkle it with a small amount rhubarb. Repeat the same steps till you use all ingredients. Put the crumble in the air fryer. Cook it at 375°F for 20 minutes.

Cinnamon Fried Plums

Prep time: 5 minutes |Cook time: 20 minutes |Serves 6

- 6 plums, cut into wedges
- 1 teaspoon ginger, ground
- ½ teaspoon cinnamon powder
- zest of 1 lemon, grated
- 2 tablespoons water
- 10 drops stevia

1. In a pan that fits the air fryer, combine the plums with the rest of the ingredients, toss gently, put the pan in the air fryer and cook at 360 °F for 20 minutes.
2. Serve cold.

Banana Beignets

Prep time: 5 minutes | Cook time: 8 minutes | Serves 6

- 1 cup almond flour
- 1/3 teaspoon nutmeg, freshly grated
- ½ teaspoon lemon juice
- 3 eggs
- ½ tablespoon baking powder
- 2 tablespoons Truvia for baking
- 1 teaspoon ground cloves
- 1/3 cup milk
- 1 ½ large-sized over-ripe bananas, peeled and sliced
- ½ teaspoon lemon peel, grated
- A pinch of turmeric

1. In a bowl drizzle banana slices with lemon juice.
2. In another bowl, combine the dry ingredients.
3. In second bowl, combine all the wet ingredients.
4. Add the wet mixture to the dry and combine well.
5. Dip each banana slice into batter.

6. Air-fry for 8-minutes at 335°F working in batches.

Plum Delight

Prep time: 5 minutes | Cook time: 18 minutes | Serves 8

- 3 eggs
- 1/3 teaspoon pure hazelnut extract
- 2 tablespoons Truvia for baking
- 1/3 cup almond flour
- A pinch of salt
- 1 ½ cups plums, pitted and halved
- 1/3 cup heavy cream

1. Firstly, butter 2 mini pie pans.
2. Lay the plum halves on the bottoms of pans.
3. In a saucepan, over medium heat, warm the milk and heavy cream until well heated.
4. Remove the pan from heat.
5. Mix in the flour using a wire whisk.
6. In a bowl, whisk the eggs, along with Truvia and salt until creamy.
7. Whisk in the creamy milk mixture.
8. Pour mixture over the plums.
9. Bake at 335°F for about 18-minutes.

Creamed Peach & Almond Dessert

Prep time: 10 minutes | Cook time: 38 minutes | Serves 6

- 6 peaches, pitted and halved
- 1/3 almonds, chopped
- well-chilled heavy cream to serve
- 1 teaspoon pure vanilla extract
- coconut oil spray for pan
- 2 tablespoons truvia for baking
- 1 teaspoon candied ginger

1. Firstly, spray baking pan with coconut oil spray; lower the peaches onto bottom of pan. In a bowl, combine almonds, Truvia, vanilla, candied ginger.
2. Scrape this mixture into the baking dish over the peaches. Bake at 380°F for 38-minutes. Garnish dessert with heavy cream.

Lemon Berries Stew

Prep time:10 minutes |Cook time: 20 minutes |Serves 4

- 1 pound strawberries, halved
- 4 tablespoons stevia
- 1 tablespoon lemon juice
- 1 and ½ cups water

1. In a pan that fits your air fryer, mix all the ingredients, toss, put it in the fryer and cook at 340 °F for 20 minutes.
2. Divide the stew into cups and serve cold.

Whipped Cream Cake

Prep time:15 minutes |Cook time: 25 minutes |Serves 12

- 1 cup almond flour
- ½ cup coconut flour
- ¼ cup coconut oil, melted
- 3 eggs, beaten
- 1 teaspoon baking powder
- 1 teaspoon vanilla extract
- 1 teaspoon cream cheese
- 2 tablespoons Splenda
- ½ cup whipped cream

1. In the mixing bowl mix up almond flour, coconut flour, coconut oil, eggs, baking powder, vanilla extract, and cream cheese.
2. Whisk the mixture well with the help of the immersion blender.
3. Then line the air fryer baking pan with baking paper.
4. Pour the cake batter in the baking pan.
5. Preheat the air fryer to 355°F.
6. Put the baking pan in the air fryer and cook it for 25 minutes.
7. Then cool the cake well.
8. Meanwhile, mix up Splenda and whipped cream cheese.
9. Spread the cake with whipped cream mixture.

Pumpkin Spices Muffins

**Prep time: 15 minutes | Cook time: 10 minutes
|Serves 6**

- 1 cup coconut flour
- 1 tablespoon pumpkin spices
- ½ teaspoon baking powder
- 2 eggs, beaten
- 2 tablespoons coconut oil
- 2 tablespoons Erythritol
- 1 tablespoon coconut cream

1. Mix all ingredients in the mixing bowl.
2. When the batter is smooth, pour it in the muffin molds and transfer in the air fryer basket.
3. Cook the muffins at 365°F for 10 minutes.

Baked Plum Cream

**Prep time: 5 minutes |Cook time: 20 minutes
|Serves 4**

- 1 pound plums, pitted and chopped
- ¼ cup swerve
- 1 tablespoon lemon juice
- 1 and ½ cups heavy cream

1. In a bowl, mix all the ingredients and whisk really well.
2. Divide this into 4 ramekins, put them in the air fryer and cook at 340 °F for 20 minutes. Serve cold.

Egg Custard

**Prep time: 5 minutes | Cook time: 30 minutes
|Serves 6**

- 6 eggs, beaten
- 2 cups heavy cream
- ½ cup Erythritol
- 1 teaspoon vanilla extract

1. Whisk all ingredients until smooth and pour in the air fryer basket.
2. Cook the custard at 345 °F for 30 minutes.
3. Then cool it well.

Vinegar Cake

**Prep time: 25 minutes |Cook time: 30 minutes
|Serves 4**

- 2 teaspoons cream cheese
- 1 teaspoon truvia
- 1 teaspoon vanilla extract
- ½ cup heavy cream
- 1 egg, beaten
- 1 teaspoon baking powder
- 1 teaspoon apple cider vinegar
- 1 ½ cup coconut flour
- 2 tablespoons butter, softened
- cooking spray

1. Pour heavy cream in the bowl. Add vanilla extract, egg, baking powder, apple cider vinegar, and butter. Stir the liquid until homogenous. Then add coconut flour.
2. Whisk the liquid until smooth. Spray the pound cake mold with cooking spray. Pour the pound cake batter in the mold.
3. Flatten its surface with the help of the spatula. Preheat the air fryer to 365°F.
4. Put the mold with the pound cake in the air fryer and cook it for 30 minutes. When the cake is cooked, cool it to the room temperature.
5. Meanwhile, in the shallow bowl whisk together cream cheese and Trivia. Then spread the surface of the pound cake with sweet cream cheese. Slice the dessert on the servings.

Vanilla Pancake Cups

Prep time: 25 minutes | Cook time:25 minutes |Serves 4

- 1/2 cup flour
- 2 eggs
- 1/3 cup coconut milk
- 1 tablespoon coconut oil, melted
- 1 teaspoon vanilla paste
- 1/4 teaspoon ground cinnamon
- A pinch of ground cardamom

1. Mix all the ingredients until well combined.
2. Let the batter stand for 20 minutes. Spoon the batter into a greased muffin tin.
3. Cook at 330 °F for 4 to 5 minutes or until golden brown. Serve with toppings of choice.
4. Bon appétit!

Mini Raspberry Tarts

Prep time: 10 minutes | Cook time: 10 minutes | Serves 8

- 1 ½ tablespoons melted coconut oil
- 16 frozen tart shells, baked

For The Filling:
- 3 tablespoons orange juice
- 1 teaspoon ground cinnamon
- 1 teaspoon ground star anise
- 1 ½ tablespoons truvia for baking
- 2 cups fresh raspberries
- 1 ½ tablespoons cornstarch
- 1 teaspoon nutmeg, grated

1. To make the filling, simmer all the filling ingredients over medium heat in a saucepan; simmer until raspberries burst and the juices have thickened.
2. Divide the filling among the tart shells with the melted coconut oil. Air-fry at

365°F for 10-minutes.

Chocolate Chip Cupcakes

Prep time: 20 minutes | Cook time: 15 minutes |Serves 6

- 3/4 cup plain flour
- 1/2 teaspoon baking powder
- 1/4 cup cocoa powder
- 3/4 cup caster sugar
- 1 egg, whisked
- 2 ounces butter, at room temperature
- 3/4 cup whole milk
- 2 ounces chocolate chips
- 1/2 teaspoon vanilla extract

1. Start by preheating your Air Fryer to 330 °F.
2. Mix all the ingredients in a bowl. Scrape the batter into silicone baking molds and place them in the Air Fryer basket.
3. Bake your cupcakes for about 15 minutes or until a tester comes out dry and clean.
4. Allow the cupcakes to cool before unmolding and serving. Bon appétit!

Chocolate Mini Cheesecakes

Prep time: 15 minutes | Cook time: 18 minutes | Serves 8

For the crust:
- 1/3 teaspoon nutmeg, grated
- 1 tablespoon Truvia
- ½ cup graham cracker crumbs
- 1 ½ tablespoons melted butter
- 1 teaspoon ground cinnamon
- A pinch of salt

For the Cheesecake:
- 2 eggs
- 1 ½ cups chocolate chips
- 1 ½ tablespoons sour cream
- 1 package soft cheese
- 2 tablespoons Truvia for baking
- ½ teaspoon vanilla essence

1. Firstly, line eight cups of mini muffin pan with paper liners.
2. To make the crust, mix the graham cracker crumbs together with 1 tablespoon Truvia, cinnamon, nutmeg, and salt.
3. Now, add the melted butter to moisten the crumb mixture.
4. Divide the crumb mixture among the muffin cups and press gently to make even layers.
5. In another bowl, whip the soft cheese, sour cream and 2 tablespoons Truvia until smooth.
6. Fold the eggs and vanilla essence in to the mix.
7. Divide half of the chocolate chips among the prepared muffin cups.
8. Then, add the cheese mix to each muffin cup.
9. Place another layer using remaining chocolate chips.
10. Bake for 18-minutes at 345°F.
11. Bake in batches, if needed.
12. To finish, transfer mini cheesecakes to a cooling rake.

Squash Fried Cake

Prep time: 15 minutes | Cook time: 10 minutes |Serves 4

- 2 cups butternut squash, shredded
- 1/2 cup all-purpose flour
- 2 eggs, beaten
- 1 tablespoon coconut oil
- 1 teaspoon pumpkin pie spice mix

1. In a mixing bowl, thoroughly combine all the ingredients.
2. Drop a spoonful of batter onto the greased Air Fryer pan. Cook in the preheated Air Fryer at 360 °F for 10 minutes, flipping them halfway through the cooking time.
3. Repeat with the remaining batter and serve warm. Enjoy!

Appendix 1 Measurement Conversion Chart

Volume Equivalents (Dry)

US STANDARD	METRIC (APPROXIMATE)
1/8 teaspoon	0.5 mL
1/4 teaspoon	1 mL
1/2 teaspoon	2 mL
3/4 teaspoon	4 mL
1 teaspoon	5 mL
1 tablespoon	15 mL
1/4 cup	59 mL
1/2 cup	118 mL
3/4 cup	177 mL
1 cup	235 mL
2 cups	475 mL
3 cups	700 mL
4 cups	1 L

Volume Equivalents (Liquid)

US STANDARD	US STANDARD (OUNCES)	METRIC (APPROXIMATE)
2 tablespoons	1 fl.oz.	30 mL
1/4 cup	2 fl.oz.	60 mL
1/2 cup	4 fl.oz.	120 mL
1 cup	8 fl.oz.	240 mL
1 1/2 cup	12 fl.oz.	355 mL
2 cups or 1 pint	16 fl.oz.	475 mL
4 cups or 1 quart	32 fl.oz.	1 L
1 gallon	128 fl.oz.	4 L

Temperatures Equivalents

FAHRENHEIT(F)	CELSIUS(C) APPROXIMATE
225 °F	107 °C
250 °F	120 ° °C
275 °F	135 °C
300 °F	150 °C
325 °F	160 °C
350 °F	180 °C
375 °F	190 °C
400 °F	205 °C
425 °F	220 °C
450 °F	235 °C
475 °F	245 °C
500 °F	260 °C

Weight Equivalents

US STANDARD	METRIC (APPROXIMATE)
1 ounce	28 g
2 ounces	57 g
5 ounces	142 g
10 ounces	284 g
15 ounces	425 g
16 ounces (1 pound)	455 g
1.5 pounds	680 g
2 pounds	907 g

Appendix 2 The Dirty Dozen and Clean Fifteen

The Environmental Working Group (EWG) is a nonprofit, nonpartisan organization dedicated to protecting human health and the environment Its mission is to empower people to live healthier lives in a healthier environment. This organization publishes an annual list of the twelve kinds of produce, in sequence, that have the highest amount of pesticide residue-the Dirty Dozen-as well as a list of the fifteen kinds ofproduce that have the least amount of pesticide residue-the Clean Fifteen.

THE DIRTY DOZEN	

The 2016 Dirty Dozen includes the following produce. These are considered among the year's most important produce to buy organic:

Strawberries	Spinach
Apples	Tomatoes
Nectarines	Bell peppers
Peaches	Cherry tomatoes
Celery	Cucumbers
Grapes	Kale/collard greens
Cherries	Hot peppers

The Dirty Dozen list contains two additional itemskale/collard greens and hot peppers-because they tend to contain trace levels of highly hazardous pesticides.

THE CLEAN FIFTEEN	

The least critical to buy organically are the Clean Fifteen list. The following are on the 2016 list:

Avocados	Papayas
Corn	Kiw
Pineapples	Eggplant
Cabbage	Honeydew
Sweet peas	Grapefruit
Onions	Cantaloupe
Asparagus	Cauliflower
Mangos	

Some of the sweet corn sold in the United States are made from genetically engineered (GE) seedstock. Buy organic varieties of these crops to avoid GE produce.

Appendix 3 Index

Elizabeth S. Levesque

Manufactured by Amazon.ca
Acheson, AB

12193995R00046